Writing IN Math Class

Writing IN Math Class

A Resource for Grades 2–8

by Marilyn Burns

MATH SOLUTIONS PUBLICATIONS

Editorial direction by Lorri Ungaretti
Design and production by Aileen Friedman
Cover illustration by Gordon Silveria

Printed in the United States of America

ISBN 0-941355-13-6

Distributed by Cuisenaire Company of America, Inc.
P.O. Box 5026
White Plains, NY 10602-5026
(800) 237-3142

Marilyn Burns Education Associates is dedicated to improving mathematics education.
For information about Math Solutions courses, resource materials, and services,
write or call:
Marilyn Burns Education Associates
150 Gate 5 Road, Suite 101
Sausalito, CA 94965
Telephone: (415) 332-4181
Fax: (415) 331-1931

Acknowledgments

Special thanks to those teachers who contributed ideas and student work.

Beth Black, Edmonds, Washington

Joan Carlson, Mendocino, California

Cathy Humphreys, San Jose, California

Joanne Lewin, San Francisco, California

Doug Nunn, Mendocino, California

Annette Raphel, Milton, Massachusetts

Cheryl Rectanus, Portland, Oregon

Cheri Schuricht, Edmonds, Washington

Stephanie Sheffield, Houston, Texas

Dee Uyeda, Mill Valley, California

LuAnn Weynand, San Antonio, Texas

Lynne Zolli, San Francisco, California

Contents

Foreword

When I tell people that Marilyn Burns's work has informed and inspired my teaching for more than twenty years, they wonder how that is possible. After all, for most of my teaching I have taught reading and junior high language arts.

In 1972, I was a K–6 remedial reading teacher, and I came across two teacher resources that challenged and transformed my pedagogy. One was a small Elementary Science Study teacher's guide for a unit called *Structures* that said, simply, that children need time and space to mess around with big ideas. The other was a small resource book of dynamic math explorations called *Good Time Mathematics*. Marilyn Burns, the author of that book, said three things that transformed my attitude about mathematics, about remedial reading, and about teaching. Marilyn said that mathematics is a way of looking at the world, that the tools of mathematics—division, fractions, and all that—are more easily understood when they're seen as part of something familiar in our lives, and that mathematics explorations can be fun.

Those two small publications have stayed by my side for more than two decades—through five schools and four states. I emphasize their smallness because we teachers who want to change the way we do things need glimpses of different terrain, not detailed road maps. We need explorers to send us beautiful postcards showing other landscapes, other possibilities for children and curriculum. We do not need manuals that take us step by step through a packaged curriculum tour, teacher guides so mammoth they should be issued with wheels.

Writing in Math Class provides us with postcards from Marilyn and the children in her care. Through their writing, children give us glimpses of their thinking. Through her commentary, Marilyn gives us glimpses of her own thinking. We see that a master teacher makes mistakes, that a master is always learning.

In *Writing in Math Class* Marilyn reveals the tentativeness of good teaching. She tells us how she learned to let her students know why she asks them to write. By letting the reader look over her shoulder as she explains "why" to her students, she articulates good pedagogy for us too.

As she looks at student writing, Marilyn reminds herself—and her readers—that partial understanding is part of learning, that children need time and space to learn new things; they need multiple and diverse experiences. I savor Marilyn's articulation of the fact that a teacher's understanding is also partial, that teachers, too, need time and space to learn new things.

Through many samples of student writing, Marilyn shows us how she responds to specific content, how she encourages her students to write more and to provide details. There are no road maps. Marilyn does not provide formulas. Through her many examples Marilyn shows us that there's no one right way to respond to students' writing. "We need to examine and assess our choices so we continue to grow in our abilities to help children learn," she writes.

Marilyn recommends addressing the purposes of assignments up front and not waiting for students to ask questions. "They need to hear why I feel it's important to make writing part of their math assignments." In letting students know that she is the eager audience for their writing, that reading their writing helps her be a better teacher, Marilyn avoids what education researcher Frank Smith calls the "arbitrariness" of most school work.

By now, it is probably plain that I like *Writing in Math Class* as much for what it reveals about teachers as for what it reveals about students. Marilyn Burns proclaims herself as a teacher, as the catalyst for student inquiry; she offers no apologies to the facilitators. Marilyn points out that a careful examination of her students' writing reveals that "Despite our best teaching efforts, the taught curriculum and the experienced curriculum are not always the same." Throughout the manuscript we hear this teacher say, "I learned."

Susan Ohanian
April 1995

Introduction

One reason I majored in mathematics in college was that papers weren't required. Homework consisted of solving problems or proving theorems, and that was just fine with me. To my thinking, math and writing were like oil and water, subjects with little in common. And for my first 20 years as an educator, writing had no part in any of the math teaching I did.

My view of math and writing has changed completely. I can no longer imagine teaching math without making writing an integral part of students' learning. This transition occurred over a period of years and because of several experiences.

One important influence was my own personal involvement with writing. In 1974, several friends encouraged me to write *The I Hate Mathematics! Book*. Writing that book began my process of whittling away at my writing anxiety. After writing ten children's books, eight books for teachers, and numerous articles, I think I've faced my writing dragon and, in so doing, I've learned how writing can help me find out about what I know and don't know about a subject.

William Zinsser, in his book *Writing to Learn*, states it clearly: "Writing is a way to work yourself into a subject and make it your own." If writing had this benefit for me, I thought, then why not for students learning mathematics?

What clinched my commitment to making writing a part of my math teaching were the initial results I had with students. I became very excited by how writing helped students think more deeply and clearly about mathematical ideas and also about their own learning. In addition, students' writing provided a window into what they were learning, what they understood, how they approached ideas, what their misconceptions were, and how they felt about their math learning.

This book is organized into three parts. In Part 1, I provide an overview of writing in math class, addressing the current goals for mathematics instruction and explaining the benefits of writing for supporting students' learning and helping teachers assess what students understand. In Part 2, I identify four types of writing assignments for students—keeping journals or logs, solving mathematical problems, explaining mathematical ideas, and linking creative writing and math. Part 3 presents tips and suggestions for making writing an integral part of math instruction, including ways to help students write, the benefits of cooperative learning, and suggestions for giving feedback. Throughout the book, I've used examples of student writing from grades 2 through 8 to illustrate and clarify the ideas I present.

The final section of the book, on pages 183–188, addresses the questions teachers ask most frequently about writing in math class. The book ends with an appendix that lists other books in which expanded versions of some of the lessons appear.

Through examining and unraveling my ideas, analyzing the student work I've collected over the years, and then putting my ideas in writing, I feel that I've clarified my thinking about the role and benefits of integrating writing into the teaching of mathematics. Writing this book has helped me in just the way William Zinsser suggested, and I hope that this personal expression will encourage other teachers to have student writing become an integral part of their math classes as well.

Part 1

WHY STUDENTS SHOULD WRITE IN MATH CLASS

The movement in education for "writing across the curriculum" calls for writing to be an integral part of teaching all subjects. Writing should no longer be limited to the language arts curriculum but instead be used as a tool to help students think about ideas in all content areas. This movement is not new to education, yet progress has been slow.

Progress has been particularly slow in the area of mathematics. Mathematics is seen as a subject that communicates through the manipulation of symbols in orderly ways, not as one that uses words to express ideas. This view is unfortunate—and misleading.

The process of writing requires gathering, organizing, and clarifying thoughts. It demands finding out what you know and don't know. It calls for thinking clearly. Similarly, doing mathematics depends on gathering, organizing, and clarifying thoughts, finding out what you know and don't know, and thinking clearly. Although the final representation of a mathematical pursuit looks very different from the final product of a writing effort, the mental journey is, at its base, the same—making sense of an idea and presenting it effectively.

In this book, I draw on my classroom experiences and those reported by other teachers to address how writing can be used in math class. I do not intend to present writing as the new answer for improving the teaching of mathematics. Teaching mathematics (or any subject) effectively is too complex for a one-dimensional approach.

This section of the book describes how writing can assist math instruction in two ways—by helping children make sense of mathematics and by helping teachers understand what children are learning.

Goals for Mathematics Instruction

In March 1989, the National Council of Teachers of Mathematics published the *Curriculum and Evaluation Standards for School Mathematics*, setting the direction for reform in the teaching and learning of mathematics. The *Standards* presents five general goals for all students: "(1) that they learn to value mathematics, (2) that they become confident in their ability to do mathematics, (3) that they become mathematical problem solvers, (4) that they learn to communicate mathematically, and (5) that they learn to reason mathematically" (page 5).

Since then, a great deal of attention and effort has been made across the country to improve how mathematics is taught. The reform movement in mathematics education has resulted in broadening the scope of the curriculum, accompanied by the development of new curriculum materials and new approaches to assessing what students are learning.

Students' early school experiences with learning mathematics are critical for forming their basic attitudes and understandings. During the elementary grades, they must develop an appreciation for and interest in mathematics, learn to think and reason mathematically, and be prepared to face new mathematical challenges.

Traditionally, the primary goal for elementary school mathematics was a narrow one—to develop student competency with arithmetic skills. Students spent the bulk of their instructional time in math class learning arithmetic procedures and practicing them on worksheets or textbook exercises. Word problems were the usual vehicle for applying these skills, presenting situations for students to translate into arithmetic sentences and then do the appropriate computations. The emphasis was on getting right answers; the teacher or the answer key was usually the source for judging whether answers were correct.

The consequences of this approach were brought to light by research results from nationwide testing. In June 1988, the Educational Testing Service released a document titled *The Mathematics Report Card: Are We Measuring Up?* The answer was a clear, resounding no! The findings documented a critical lack of effective reasoning skills among the nation's students. As reported: "Few youngsters can put mathematics to work effectively in solving everyday problems, and such practical activity is absent from most classrooms." The situation was described as dismal.

Reflections from Middle School Students

Students' writing can reveal how they view their mathematics instruction. On the first day of class, Cathy Humphreys asked her seventh and eighth grade students in San Jose, California, to write math autobiographies about their elementary school math experiences. These students had received traditional math instruction in the elementary grades. The following samples were typical of the more than 100 papers Cathy received.

Jamie wrote: *So far in my math classes, I have learned addition, subtraction, multiplication, division, etc. . . . all the basic things. For example: I remember 2nd grade—Mrs. _____'s class. We had all come in from snack time. She was trying to teach us how to multiply. I remember getting so frustrated on learning what 9 × 9 equaled! I finally understood it. Then what hits us . . . division! That took longer to learn, but I got it after a lot of help from my dad.*

From Ed: *When I first studied math I kind of liked it because it was very easy. All we had to do was add and subtract. But the numbers got bigger over the years and I didn't have enough fingers. But then it got easy again because I did multiplication tables up to twelve and I memorized them very quick and I was one of the best in the class. When fifth grade came I still was good because division was very easy too. But when I got to sixth and seventh grade, I was kind of in the middle because I was too afraid to ask questions, and I got C's and B minuses on my report card. Now in my 8th grade I'm not sure because its only the first day.*

Craig wrote: *I started doing math in the first grade. When we first started I did okay. Later on we did double digit adding. I didn't like it very much so I hid my work in my math folder. Later my teacher found it and made me do the work.*

When I was in the third grade we had to take math tests. We had one minute to do fifty problems. Each time we passed we did a harder test. Eventually we took a test of one-hundred problems. At the end of the report period my mom had a conference with my teacher. She noticed I got 100% on my math tests. At an assembly they gave me a certificate of achievment.

My Math Autobiography

I started doing math in the first grade. When we first started I did okay. Later on we did double digit adding. I didn't like it very much so I hid my work in my math folder. Later my teacher found it and made me do the work.

When I was in the the Third grade we had to take math tests. We had one minute to do fifty problems. Each time we passed we did a harder test. Eventually we took a test of one-hundred problems. At the end of the report period my mom had a conference with my teacher. She noticed I got 100% on my math tests. At an assembly they gave me a certificate of achievment.

Craig recalled his elementary math experience as only learning arithmetic. (Grade 7)

Alisa wrote: *In 3rd grade I had a teacher named Miss _____. I only remember one thing. One day we were doing times tables. She called on me to stand up and say the 2's. Well I stud up and started. I said 2 × 1. And I couldn't remember anymore and I stud up there trying to remember and then I was so embaressed I started to cry. She let me sit down and she told me to stop crying. Thats all I remember about 3rd grade. In 4th my teacher gave us a sheet of paper with times tables already on it. She gave us 1 minite to do as many as we could. I never did them all, but I tryed. In 5th, Mrs. _____ gave us a longer sheet with times tables on it already but she gave us 3 minites to do it. Thats all I remember.*

Allen's feelings were mixed, but he generally felt positive about math. He wrote: *Math has always been my favorite subject in school. My favorite thing about math are word problems because they are so challenging to do. I also like fractions. I remember how much I liked solving fraction problems in 4th grade.*

The thing about math that I did not like was long division. The reason I did not like it was because I did not really understand it. The feeling about that was terrible.

In all my years I [in] school I basicly really liked math. I enjoy it so much because math is like a maze in most cases. There is only one answer to it.

> Math has always been my favorite subject in school. My favorite thing about math are word problems because they are so challenging to do. I also like fractions. I remember how much I liked solving fraction problems in 4th grade
>
> The thing about math that I did not like was long division. The reason I did not like it was because I did not really understand it. The feeling about that was terrible.
>
> In all my years I school I basicly really liked math. I enjoy it so much because math is like a maze in most cases. There is only one answer to it.

Allen generally felt positive about the math he had learned, but expressed his frustration about not understanding long division. (Grade 7)

Common to these responses is that the students equated learning mathematics with learning how to solve arithmetic problems for which there is always one right method and one right answer. For these students, it seems that the quick right answer had been valued more than the thinking that led to the answer.

Too often, children learn to compute without understanding why the computation procedures make sense. Missing from instruction has been attention to children's explaining the procedures they use, justifying their reasoning, judging the reasonableness of their solutions, and reflecting on their thinking—all those behaviors that contribute to the development of mathematical thinking and number sense.

Also missing from traditional instruction has been the opportunity to involve children in the richness of what mathematics has to offer. Mathematics is more than arithmetic. The study of mathematics, even for young children, should encompass all areas of the math curriculum—geometry, measurement, patterns and functions, probability, statistics, and algebra, as well as number. The NCTM *Standards* contains sections on each of these areas and, in the area of number, addresses number sense, estimation, and number relationships as well as computation.

In contrast to traditional instruction, current practices for effective mathematics teaching call for actively engaging children with mathematical experiences that help them make sense of mathematical ideas. Children benefit from using concrete materials, working in small groups that allow them to learn from one another, and using calculators and computers. Based on the notion that students develop understanding of math concepts by creating those understandings for themselves from their learning experiences, the *Standards* calls for increased attention to problem solving, communication, and reasoning, and for helping students to become actively involved in doing and learning mathematics.

Reflections from Third Graders

Dee Uyeda, a third grade teacher in Mill Valley, California, has been teaching mathematics in ways that are consistent with the current standards. At the end of one year, Dee asked her students to write what they had learned about math. Their papers reflected a broad view of mathematics.

Ann wrote: *I learned that math is not just adding. It is patterns, working as a group to solve problems, shapes, mathematical words, couculaters, prediting, finding out if your predictshion is right, areas of things, diescovering things about math, writing down what you discovered, geometry, big words like Equilateral, Isosceles, Scalene, right, and subtracting.*

What I Learned About Math
I learned that math is not just adding. It is patterns, working as a group to solve problems, shapes, mathematical words, couculaters, prediting, finding out if your predictshion is right, areas of things, diescovering things about math, writing down what you discovered, geometry, big words like Equilateral, Isosceles, Scalene, right, and subtracting.

Ann wrote that math was more than adding, and listed other things she had learned. (Grade 3)

Amber wrote: *This year I have learnd things in math I never thought existed.*

A few years ago math time meant working in your math book, but not any more.

This year I have learned about geometry, and what it has to do with math. When we were working on polygons a long time ago, we were trying to see how many lines we could draw to the other sides of the polygon.

Or when we were working on mirror symetry, some of the class used one mirror. Some two or three. There were always more patterns to be found.

At the begining of the year I thought that it was very important if you found a pattern, but not now. Now I know that patterns are everywhere just waiting to be found.

From Timmy: I learned how to think hard and still have fun. I also learned how to get a good strateggy. I learned that patterns were every where and that patterns are important to look for in everything you do. I

What I Learned

△ + ⊗ = This Year in Math

This year I have learnd things in math I never thought existed.

A few years ago math time meant working in your math book, but not any more.

This year I have learned about geometry, and what it has to do with math. When we were working on polygons a long time ago, we were trying to see how many lines we could draw to the other sides of the polygon.

Example:

Or when we were were working on mirron symetry, some of the class used one mirror, Some two or three. There were always more patterns to be found.

At the begining of the year I thought that it was very important if you found a pattern, but not now. Now I know that patterns are everywhere just waiting to be found.

During the year, Amber was particularly fascinated by geometry. (Grade 3) *learned that math is long and fancy words like isosceles and perpendicular. The ice cream cone problem made me learn more about statistics. Over all I learned that math is fun.*

Mairead wrote: *I lerned that numbers are very valubel. We wouldn't know how to add. And if we didn't know how to add we couldn't add prices.*

Also I think if we didn't have numbers this world wouldn't be like it is. I learned that geometry is a part of math. I learned that you can have a certen amount of length and get difrent areas inside. Measuring inches and centameters is thrilling! Sometimes measuring was hard but as I learned it got easeyer. I learned a pattern is something you can go by. I think that calculators are fun. They also help you learn. At least I had that experience. It helped me memorize my times facts.

The difference between mathematics instruction that has the goal of "doing arithmetic" and math instruction that has the goal of "doing mathematics" is substantial. Theresa, a third grader who had transferred to Dee Uyeda's class in March, described the contrast in her final paper.

She wrote: *When I first came to Park school I learned how to find the volume of thngs and more things in multiplication and division and measureing. Then I learned how to play the fraction game and learned shapes. Then I learned how to play pig. Pig was fun because you get to add and subtract. Then I learned how to find the area and use centimeters with a ruler. I learned about polygons then box filling and foot measureing.*

In _____ we learned easier things than here. Like easy multiplication and division in hard back math books and we didn't have any activities or measurement like there is here. We had our own desks and we did our math on our own.

These writing samples provide insights into students' views of mathematics and their own learning experiences. The writing was valuable for the students, as it focused them on examining their thoughts and perceptions. The information was valuable for their teachers, as it revealed the students' thinking. These samples show one way writing can be brought into the math classroom.

Using Writing to Support Learning

Incorporating writing into math class adds an important and valuable dimension to learning by doing. Writing encourages students to examine their ideas and reflect on what they have learned. It helps them deepen and extend their understanding. When students write about mathematics, they are actively involved in thinking and learning about mathematics.

The NCTM *Standards* addresses how communication in math class benefits students' learning at all grade levels. For grades K–4, the *Standards* states: "Writing is a communication skill that has been used too infrequently in mathematics" (page 28). The section also states: "Young children learn language through verbal communication; it is important, therefore, to provide opportunities for them to 'talk mathematics.' . . . Writing about mathematics, such as describing how a problem was solved, also helps students clarify their thinking and develop deeper understanding" (page 26).

The grades 5–8 section states: "Middle school students should have many opportunities to use language to communicate their mathematical ideas. . . . Opportunities to explain, conjecture, and defend one's ideas orally and in writing can stimulate deeper understandings of concepts and principles. . . . Writing and talking about their thinking clarifies students' ideas and gives the teacher valuable information from which to make instructional decisions" (pages 78–79).

Following are descriptions from three classrooms that give examples of how writing can support students' learning. In each class, the emphasis of the math instruction was on children's thinking, reasoning, and making sense of mathematical ideas.

The first vignette describes two lessons done with the same class of second graders in which the children were given a problem to solve and were asked to explain their reasoning in writing. The first lesson was done on the second day of school and the second lesson in February.

The second vignette describes a fifth grade class in which the students worked cooperatively in small groups on a problem that involved fractions. This occurred in February, after the class had been studying fractions for several weeks.

The third vignette presents sixth graders' work done in October. In this situation, the students were asked to write solutions to division word problems.

Problem Solving (Grade 2)

Helping children become comfortable with writing in math class takes time and effort. First attempts are often difficult for the children and can be discouraging for teachers. However, with encouragement and practice, children improve. Following are samples of writing from a second grade class in Mill Valley, California, which I taught for an hour each day. I've included samples from work done early in the year and then five months later.

I was interested in having the math lesson on the first day of school reflect what we would be doing throughout the year. I wanted to introduce the children to the idea that I was interested not only in their answers but also in their thinking. Also, I wanted the students to see how writing could help them think about a problem and arrive at a solution. For this first lesson, I planned to give the children a problem to solve and have them represent their thinking on paper.

I showed the class *One Gorilla* by Atsuko Morozumi, a book that won the 1990 New York Times Best Illustrated Children's Book Award. On the opening page, the author writes: "Here is a list of things I love." His story tells about one gorilla who makes his way through jungles and gardens past two butterflies, three budgerigars, four squirrels, five pandas, six rabbits, seven frogs, eight fish, nine birds, and ten cats.

After reading the book aloud, I listed on the board the numerals from 1 to 10 and asked the children to recall the animals in the book. As the children offered their ideas, I referred to the book to check and wrote the names of the animals next to the appropriate numerals.

Then I posed the problem to the children of figuring out how many animals the author loved altogether. I gave the children directions. "You can write or draw whatever will help you think about the problem," I said.

"Then write your answer and explain how you figured." To help them get started with their writing, I wrote a prompt on the board:

He loved ___ things.
I figured it out by _____.

Before distributing paper, I said, "Raise your hand if you understand the problem you're supposed to solve." About half of the students raised their hands. I asked the class to listen carefully as two children explained the problem.

Then I asked, "What are you supposed to write on your paper?" Again, I had volunteers explain. I added as reinforcement, "Write or draw on the paper whatever you need to help you think about solving the problem." I then distributed paper, and the children got to work.

The math period reflected the typical confusion of a first day at school. About half of the children got right to work. Of the rest, a few raised their hands for help. Several others began doing things that had nothing to do with the assignment—fiddling with things in their desks, drawing pictures that didn't relate to the problem, or wandering off to do something else. Gray had his head down and was gently sobbing, something he had been doing on and off all morning. Two boys argued about crayons.

I circulated, encouraging some children, refocusing others on the problem, offering help, settling disputes, listening to children's ideas, and pushing for more explanations. I tried to comfort Gray. He finally lifted his head and began to draw a dinosaur on his paper. It had nothing to do with the book, but he explained, "It's something I love."

Of the 26 children, 10 drew tally marks to help them solve the problem, although they organized the tally marks in different ways. Molly, for example, drew them in groups of 1, 2, 3, up to 10, and then counted. Leslie was one of 6 children who organized tally marks into 5s. She wrote: *I added them together.* However, she added incorrectly and got an answer of 56. When I asked Leslie about what she had written, she became confused and couldn't explain. I accepted her paper.

Seth started by making tally marks. However, he abandoned that method and instead wrote numerals: *1 22 333 4444 55555 666666 7777777 88888888 999999999 10101010101010101010.* Then he counted how many numerals he had written and changed his original answer of 47 to the correct answer of 55.

Twelve children used some combination of pictures, words, and numbers. Four were unable to make any progress on the problem. Jason's paper expressed what these four children felt: *Its to hade.* "It's too hard," he read to me.

$$6 + 4 + 9 + 15 + 21 = 62$$

I Odded them together

Leslie began to combine the tally marks; however, she became confused and arrived at the incorrect answer. (Grade 2)

Seth gave up on using tally marks and instead wrote numerals to help him count. (Grade 2)

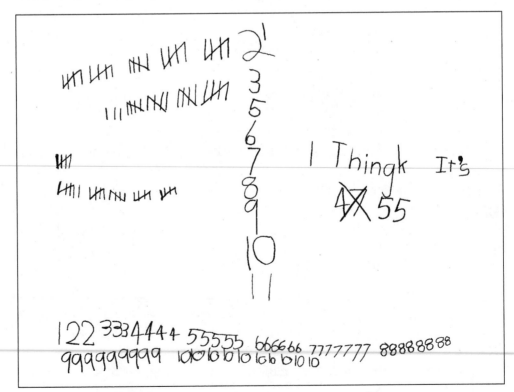

I Thingk It's 55

I counted
1
2
3
4
5
6
7
8
9
10

gorilla 1 2 3 4 5 6
7 8 9 10 11 12 13 14 15
16 17 18 19 20 21 22 23
24 25 26 27 28
fish 29 30 31 32 33
fish 34 35 36 37 38
fish 39 40 41 42 43
fish 44 45 46 47
fish 48 49 50 51
fish 52
fish 53
fish 54 55
Bird Squirrels
Bird Squirrels
Bird Squirrels
Bird Squirrels
Bird Pandas
Bird Pandas
Bird Pandas
Bird Pandas
Bird Pandas
Bird
cat cat
cat cat frog frog
cat cat frog
cat frog
cat frog
cat frog
cat frog

After writing the names of the animals, Marina counted, pointing to each word and picture with her left hand while she kept track by writing the numbers in the upper right corner of her paper. (Grade 2)

None of the children paid any attention to the prompt I had written on the board. However, I continued to offer prompts for subsequent writing assignments and found that over the year the children found them helpful some of the time and, at other times, preferred to express themselves in their own ways.

Later in the school year, during a unit on place value, I showed the class a plastic bowl and asked each student to put in two "fish." (I used Snap cubes, which the children willingly called fish.) The regular teacher, the student teacher, and I also put in two fish each, as did the music teacher, who had walked into the room to check on our schedule. I wrote on the board:

25 children
4 adults

After discussing how many people had put fish into the bowl, I posed a problem. "How many fish are in the bowl altogether?" I asked. I wrote the problem on the board:

> How many fish are in the bowl altogether?
> Explain your thinking with numbers and words.
> You may also use pictures.

The children had heard me say many times that they were to use numbers, words, and pictures. I reinforced this direction over and over throughout the year and took time to talk about it with them from time to time. I also wrote a prompt they could use to begin their explanation:

> There are ___ fish in the bowl.
> I think this because _____.

I gave the children the choice of working in pairs or alone. Only four children chose to work alone; there were nine pairs and one group of three.

Some papers showed the children's complete understanding of the problem and command over the numbers. Gwyn, for example, wrote on her and Sarah's paper: *25 + 25 = 50 + 4 + 4 = 8 + 50 = 58. There are 58 fish in the bowl. I think this because if you add 25 & 25 it is 50 and then add 8 on it is 58.*

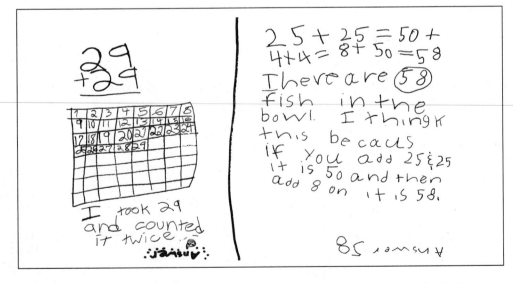

Although Sarah and Gwyn worked together, they each used half of the paper for their own solutions. Sarah wrote the numbers from 1 to 29 on a grid and counted them twice. Gwyn added in her head. (Grade 2)

"That's the longest problem I've ever written," Gwyn told me when she gave me the paper. Three other pairs of children and one child who worked alone used this same reasoning.

Rudy and Nick's paper presented a different way of explaining the answer. They wrote: *There are 58 fish in the bowl. We think this because 25 × 2 = 50 and 4 × 2 = 8 and 50 + 8 = 58.*

In my experience, using multiplication is unusual for second graders, but Rudy knew a great deal about mathematics. His partners often benefitted from his understanding.

Some children relied on a pictorial representation. Teddy and Katy, for example, drew 29 sets of two tallies. They wrote: *We think the ansar is 58 bkas* [because] *we catan* [counted]. Two other pairs of children also made drawings. Tomo and Colleen drew fish; Jonathan and Grace drew 29 trains with two cubes in each.

Teddy and Katy drew tallies in groups of two and counted them. (Grade 2)

Timmy and Jason weren't able to make sense of the problem, but they discussed it at length and worked hard on their paper. They wrote: *There are 32 fish in the bosl. I think this becuse we counted by 2 and came up 32.*

Five other children handed in work that showed their lack of understanding. Since they're free to talk with others, three of these children recorded the correct answer, but they were not able to offer any explanation, either on their papers or to me orally.

The students' work showed a range of approaches and much improvement from earlier in the year in their ability to use writing to think about problems and explain their reasoning.

Eli worked alone. He counted on by writing numbers beginning with 30. He went to 59 but realized he had written one number too many. (Grade 2)

Seth and Andrew worked together and solved the problem symbolically. (Grade 2)

Learning about Fractions (Grade 5)

Fractions is a standard topic in the fifth grade mathematics curriculum. Children are taught how to change fractions to equivalent fractions and to add, subtract, multiply, and divide with fractions. Many children get lost in the rules: To change a fraction to an equivalent fraction, multiply or divide the numerator and denominator of the fraction by the same number; to add, add the numerators but not the denominators; to multiply, multiply across the numerators and the denominators; to divide, invert the divisor and then follow the rule for multiplying. Too often, students learn and practice procedures without understanding why they work. (I remember learning as a child: Yours is not to question why, just invert and multiply.)

Stephanie Sheffield used a problem-solving approach to help her fifth graders in Houston, Texas, develop understanding of fractions. Rather than teaching the children pencil-and-paper procedures, Stephanie presented them with problems to work on in small cooperative groups. She used a variety of manipulative materials so that the children had concrete models to use and explore. And she incorporated writing into their learning activities by having them describe the reasoning they used to find solutions to the problems.

One problem Stephanie gave the class was to figure out how to share five candy bars equally among four people. The students were organized into groups of three or four. Stephanie gave each group five rectangles cut from brown construction paper to make "candy bars." She had folded each rectangle into sixths.

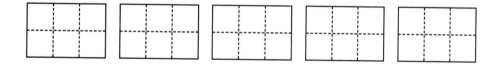

Stephanie told the class, "I folded this paper to look like chocolate candy bars that are scored into sections." Stephanie said this to give her candy bars a reference with which the children were familiar.

Stephanie asked the students to write about their work. "I would like you to explain how to share the five candy bars equally among four people," she said. In this assignment, their writing was to be a record of their thinking processes as they solved the problem.

For the last of the directions, Stephanie said, "As part of your answer, include one number that tells how much each person gets."

The children had previously worked on similar problems. Using paper circles, they had shared three, four, five, and six "cookies" among four children. When they solved the problem of dividing up five cookies, most students had given each person one cookie and then divided the last cookie into fourths. The candy bar problem was essentially the same, except that Stephanie had folded the "candy bars" into six sections each. She had the hidden agenda of seeing how the children would solve the problem of dividing the sixths among four people. Would the children ignore the folds and cut the last candy bar into four pieces? If not, what would they do with the extra sections? And how would they represent their answer numerically?

Just as Stephanie had suspected, the children's writing gave insights into their reasoning processes. Tanya, John, Janice, and Joel were excited by their discovery. They wrote: *We pass out 4 candies bars to each person. Each peron got one whole. One whole left over. We cut the candy bar into each six pieces. Then pass each out. 2 are left over. Cut the last 2 pieces into halves—pass out all 4 to each person. Each person gets 1 and ⅙ and ¹⁄₁₂. Joel says couldn't we just take our last candy bar and divide it in half and half again. John says that would be ¼. We took everybodys ⅙ piece and ¹⁄₁₂ piece and covered the 1 whole piece and found out that the ⅙ and ¹⁄₁₂ are realy ¼. 1¼ each person gets.*

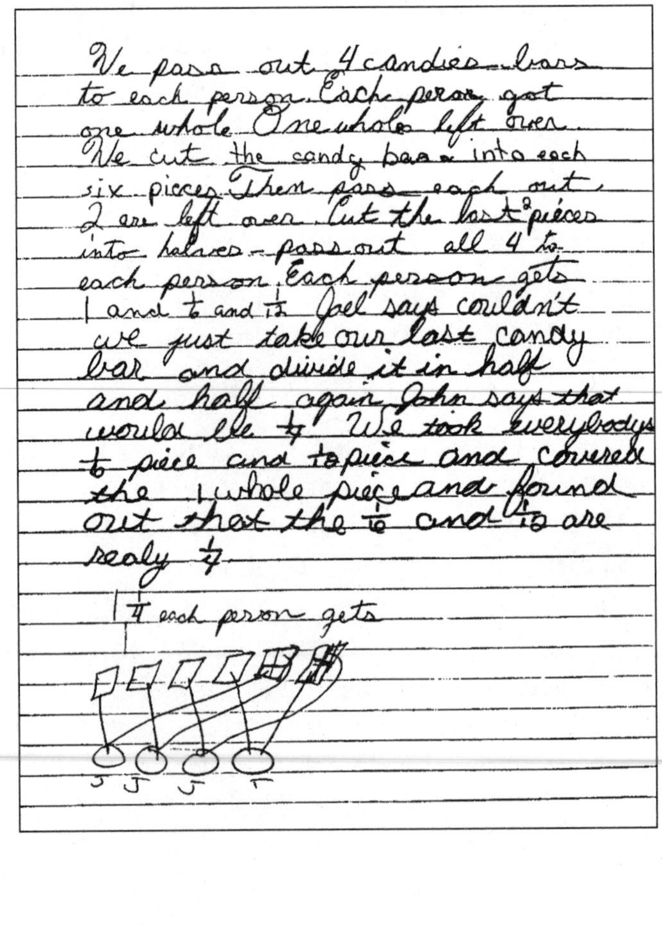

From working on the problem, Tanya, John, Janice, and Joel discovered that ¼ is the same as ⅙ and ¹⁄₁₂ combined. (Grade 5)

Katherine, Jesse, Namthong, and Miriam included their social interaction in their explanation: *First Namthong says, "I think we each get 1¼." So we tried it but first Namthong and Miriam cutted them. Then Katherine said "Divide them by 3." Namthong checked to see if everybody had equal parts. Jesse said, "I think we each get 1³⁄₆." Katherine said "³⁄₆ = ½ so that means 1½." Namthong said "We have 1⅓." Katherine and Namthong started arguing about the answer while Miriam and Jesse were fooling around. Katherine and Namthong tried it out while Jesse and Miriam were playing. Finally Katherine and Namthong figured it out by themselves. We made a mistake so we're starting over. We pass out the candy to each one. Namthong said "We cut down and across." Katherine said "Let say this is a whole." Katherine said "If we cut the way you did then this would happen:* [see children's work below]. *Kathrine agreed. So each of us get 1¼.*

Katherine, Jesse, Namthong, and Miriam wrote a detailed description of the process they went through to solve the problem. (Grade 5)

Linda, Lawren, and David solved the problem, but didn't represent their answer as one number correctly. They wrote: *Everyone got one whole candy bar. Everyone gets ⅙ of a candy bar. Everyone gets ²⁄₂₄ of a candy bar. That is how we divided our five candy bars with four people. We each got* $^{30}/_{120}$. *They also wrote* $1 + \frac{1}{6} + \frac{2}{24}$ *on their paper.*

The children's answer of $^{30}/_{120}$ does not make sense by itself. However, when considered in light of the reasoning they presented on their paper, it can be explained. They divided each candy bar into 24 pieces and multiplied that by 5 to get 120 pieces for all the candy bars together. Then they divided 120 by 4 to get 30. So each person gets 30 of the 120 pieces, or $^{30}/_{120}$ of the five candy bars.

From approaching a new concept in this way, with a focus on expressing their thinking through writing, children learn that they have the ability to face new problems and work their way to solutions. They learn that being able to explain a procedure is as important as being able to apply it. They learn to think and reason with fractions, not merely to memorize and practice. Also, writing gives them a way to revisit their thinking, which can help reinforce their understanding.

Division Word Problems (Grade 6)

LuAnn Weynand found that her middle school students in San Antonio, Texas, often entered her class with a variety of understandings—and mis-understandings—about division. Included in LuAnn's teaching goals for division was that her students would be able to relate division to real-life situations, find the answers to division problems in more than one way, and make sense of remainders.

Early in the year, LuAnn presented the class with a division story problem she had written. She organized the class into small groups and displayed the following directions on an overhead transparency:

1. Show how to solve the problem in two ways.
2. Express the remainder in a way that makes sense.
3. Explain your reasoning.

After groups had completed the assignment, they reported to the class what they had written, explaining the different division methods they had used and how they had expressed remainders. This introductory lesson provided the students with a model of a division story problem, showed them a variety of methods for solving the problem, and brought their attention to ways of representing the remainder.

LuAnn then had each group write a division story problem for others to solve. She put the problems on overhead transparencies and used them for subsequent lessons. For each problem, LuAnn had the students follow the same directions they had followed for her problem. In each lesson, groups presented their work to the class for discussion.

One group wrote the following story: *Mrs. Weynand wanted to have a Halloween festival but her house was too small. She thought and thought for many days. Then it finally got to her mind. She wanted to rent a big hall. The rent for one night was $85. She estimated $2 per each person. How many people does she have to invite to cover the cost?*

One group answered: *Ms. Weynand had to invite 42 people and she had to pay a dollar.*

If Ms. Weynand didn't want to pay a dollar she would have to invite another person.

We can't report the remader as a fraction because we can't cut a person in half.

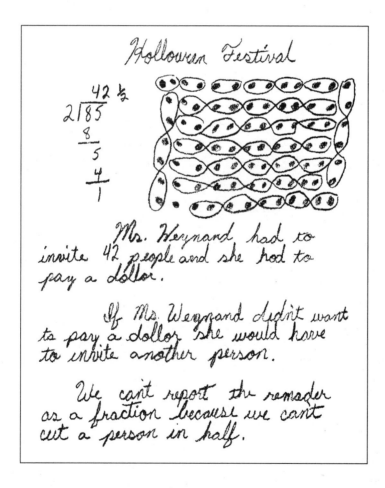

After dividing, this group gave two suggestions and explained why they could not report the remainder as a fraction. (Grade 6)

Another group changed 85 to 86 to avoid the problem of getting a remainder when dividing by 2. They wrote: *Mrs. Weynand had to invite 43 people to cover the cost. Each person has to pay 2 dollars.*

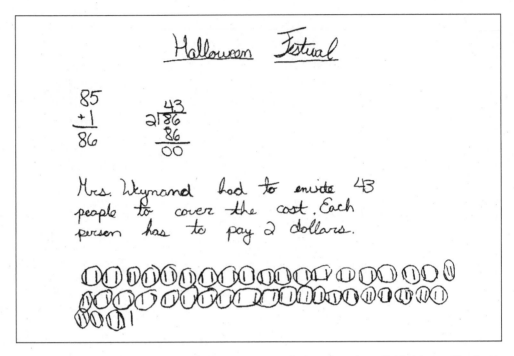

This group changed 85 to 86 to avoid getting a remainder when they divided by 2. (Grade 6)

Another group also came up with 43 people, but explained the answer in a different way: *Mrs. Weynand has to invite 43 people to the Halloween festival. You shouldn't use a fraction because you can't invite a half of a person. You shouldn't just invite 42 people because you would be one dollar short.*

One group presented two possible solutions: *Mrs. Weynand has to invite 43 people to cover the charge. She can use the extra $1.00 for Jolly Wrancher candy. Mrs. Weynand can invite 42 people and a baby to cover the full charge of $85.*

In a problem written by a different group, the remainder could sensibly be represented as a fraction: *Mrs. Weynand was having a party. She went to the store to buy some cookies. She bought a box of cookies that contained 125 cookies. She has 20 guests. How many cookies can each guest get?*

One group's response was typical of the answers the students produced: *Each person could have 6 and ¼ cookies and each person could get 6 cookies with 5 left over. Your remainder should be reported by a fraction because you can divide cookies into fractions.*

Another group also produced a numerical answer of 6¼. However, the students offered an alternative solution that avoided the remainder, yet still made sense in the context of the situation: *15 guest can get 6 cookies and 5 guest can get 7 cookies.*

One group used repeated subtraction to figure the answer and also used division notation to represent the problem. They wrote: *Each guests can get 6¼ cookies.*

After drawing 125 dots to represent the cookies, these students grouped them into 20s. They represented the answer with a fraction, but suggested another solution for actually sharing the cookies. (Grade 6)

This group used repeated subtraction to figure the answer. The students also used the division notation to represent the problem. (Grade 6)

LuAnn feels that having the students work in small groups is beneficial. In these lessons, students talked about division and remainders and learned from one another. Some were able to share the knowledge they had; others had gaps in their understanding filled.

Using Writing to Assess Understanding

Writing not only benefits children by contributing to their learning, it benefits teachers by helping them assess what their students are learning. Since I've been using writing as an integral part of my math teaching, I've found that I have information about students' understanding that I didn't have access to before. Rather than merely presenting answers to problems, students' writing also provides insights into how they think and reason mathematically. When I read what students have written, I have a broader awareness of what they understand as well as what they're able to do.

Assessing is best done in the context of classroom learning and when integrated into the instructional program. Activities assigned primarily for assessment should be no different in quality from other learning activities. That is, they should be assignments that require students to solve problems, reflect on mathematical ideas, use mathematical language and notation, and explain their thinking and reasoning. The only difference with an assignment given for assessment is that teachers look at the results to learn about what students understand and how they apply mathematical ideas to a variety of situations.

Students' writing can serve three assessment purposes. First, reading students' papers helps teachers evaluate how well the instructional program is supporting learning goals. The following sorts of questions help teachers evaluate the general effectiveness of their instructional choices:

- What have the students learned?
- Was the reasoning shown by the class strong, adequate, or weak?

- Are students using the mathematics presented during class lessons?
- Do lessons provide opportunities for learning that challenge the more interested and capable students while also being accessible to students with less aptitude for math?
- Are there noticeable gaps in understanding or information?

In general, students' papers provide feedback and direction that provide teachers with useful information for thinking about changing, refining, and enhancing instructional choices.

Second, students' writing is also important for learning about individuals' understanding and skills. Reading students' writing can provide valuable clues to the kinds of experiences that might be beneficial to particular individuals, not with the goal of "fixing" or remediating children, but in the spirit of providing additional opportunities to help them make sense of mathematics and develop understanding of mathematical ideas and skills. Partial understanding and confusion are natural to the process of learning, and students need ample experiences to broaden and deepen their understanding.

Third, students' writing provides an excellent vehicle for communicating with parents about what their children are learning and the progress they're making. What students write is an effective resource, both for parent conferences and for organizing portfolios.

It's important to point out that students' writing should not be the only vehicle for assessing their learning. In the classroom, teachers learn about what students know from listening to what they say during whole class discussions, observing and listening as they work on activities, conversing with individual students, as well as reading their written work. Students' writing is particularly beneficial for assessment, however, as it provides a concrete way to review and revisit their thinking and reflect on what they are learning.

Following are descriptions from four classrooms that offer examples of how writing can be helpful for assessing what students understand. The first example concerns work from the second graders described on pages 14–20 and shows how they approached a situation that required them to compare two-digit numbers. The second example is from a third grade class and describes an assignment given near the end of a unit on division. In the third example, results are presented from one of the problems in a fifth grade assessment on fractions. The fourth example describes two assignments about percents given to a class of seventh and eighth grade students.

Comparing Numbers (Grade 2)

This work was done in March when I was teaching a unit to second graders on combining and comparing numbers. At this time of the year, I was enjoying the payoff from the work I had done with the class since September. The children approached problem situations with interest and confidence and willingly explained their reasoning processes, and their work gave an indication of the improvement in their writing ability. (See pages 14–17 for examples of work from this same class earlier in the year.)

For this lesson, I had put Snap cubes into five identical plastic jars, putting just one color in each jar. I showed all five jars to the class and then chose the ones with blue cubes and white cubes. The jar with blue cubes was filled to the top; the jar with white cubes was approximately half full.

"How many blue cubes do you think are in this jar?" I said, holding it up for the children to see. Many of them were willing to venture guesses, and their guesses ranged from 10 to 123. I removed cubes from the jar, one at a time, snapping them together until I had made a train of 10.

"Look at how full the jar is now," I said, "and decide if you'd like to change your estimates." The jar was more than half full of blue cubes. Some children changed their guesses. Others didn't, but the range of their estimates narrowed. Their estimates now went from 20 to 100. I removed 10 more cubes and made another train. The jar now was about half full.

"How many cubes do you now think are in the jar?" I asked. I noticed which children made reasonable estimates and which didn't. I made a third train of 10, leaving 6 blue cubes in the jar. The children figured out that there were 36 cubes altogether. I put the cubes back into the jar and wrote on the board:

Blue cubes—36

I then took the jar that was half full of white cubes and held it up for the children to see. Again, I had children estimate. This time, I asked each child who volunteered an estimate to explain why his or her estimate made sense. Responses ranged from "I think 20 because it looks a little more than half full" to "I think 25 because I just think that."

After all the children who wanted to had offered their ideas, I emptied the jar to count the white cubes. There were 19. I returned the cubes to the jar and wrote on the board:

White cubes—19

Then I posed a problem to the students. I asked, "How many more white cubes would we have to add to this jar so it would have as many cubes as the jar with blue cubes?" Some students immediately raised their hands.

"For this question, I don't want you to make a guess," I said. "I'd like you to think about it and figure out how many cubes we need to add. Then I'd like you to write about how you reasoned." I wrote on the board:

<u>The Blue and White Cube Problem</u>
We have to put in ___ more white cubes because _____.

Before the children began work, I gave my usual reminder: "To explain your reasoning, use words, numbers, and, if you'd like, pictures."

The children had been involved in solving problems and explaining their reasoning for six months, and the purposeful atmosphere in the class as they worked and the ease with which most children wrote showed the growth they had made. Their papers reflected the many different ways they approached the problem.

Some children counted on from 19 to 36. Rudy, for example wrote the numbers from 19 to 36. He wrote a small 1 over the 20, a 2 over the 21, continuing until he had written 17 over the 36. He wrote: *I think it is 17.*

Rudy solved the problem by counting on from 19 to 36, carefully numbering to get the answer. (Grade 2)

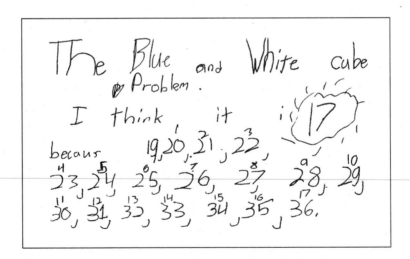

Leslie was one of two children who counted backward from 36 to 19. She did it correctly, but commented to me, "It's hard to count backwards. I'll never do it that way again!"

Some children used trial and error, adding a number to 19 and then adjusting. Catherine, for example, wrote: *We have to put in 17. I picked 17 because I counted and first I had 14 and that only got me to 33 and then I counted up from 33 to 36 and I got 17.*

the Blue + white Cube problem
We have to put in 17. I picked
17 because I Counted and
first I had 14 and that only
got me to 33 and then
I Counted up from EE to EG and
I got 17.

Catherine described how she used trial and error, starting with an estimate and then making an adjustment to get the answer. (Grade 2)

Some children had unique ways of figuring. Marina, for example, wrote: *We have to put in 17 more white cubes in the white jar because you got 19 white cubes in the white jar but how manny more to go up to 36? You got 19 white cubes plus 11 makes 30 plus six makes 17. So you need 17 more white cubes to fill the jar.*

The blue and white cube problem
We have to put in 17
more white cubes in
the white jar because
you got 19 white cubes
in the white jar but
how manny more to
go up to 36? You got
19 white Cubes plus 11 makes
30 plus six makes 17.
So you need 17 more
white cubes to fill the
jar.

Marina first figured she needed 11 more to make 30 and 6 more to make 36. Then she added 11 and 6 to get 17. (Grade 2)

Teddy wrote: *We have to put in 17 more white cubes Because you take 10 and 10 and then 10 and 10 is 20 and you have nine and 7 and you take one from the 7 and then you have onuther 10 and that is 30 and you have 6 so it is 36.*

And from Hassan: *If there are 36 blue cubes and 19 white add 1 to 19 you get 20. Add 16 you get 36. Because 19 add 1 = 20 and you add 16 if youed be 36 and thats what filled the blue jar. All together you put in 17.*

The blue + white cube problem
If there are 36 blue cubes
and 19 white add 1 to 19 you get 20.
Add 16 you get 36. Because
19 add 1=20 and you add 16 it youed be
36 and thats what filled the blue jar.
All together you put in 17.

Hassan's method was similar to Marina's, but he chose to add different numbers. (Grade 2)

When the children had solved the problem, I asked them to share their solutions by reading them aloud. My plan was to have the children compare the contents of other pairs of jars, so discussing their different solutions to this problem would give them a variety of options for thinking about comparing numbers. In this way, not only were the papers useful for my assessment, but they also contributed to the students' learning.

Comparing Raisins (Grade 5)

It's important for students both to learn to apply number skills to problem-solving situations and to learn that there is more than one way to solve a problem. In this lesson, I presented fifth graders with a problem that was created by Annette Raphel, a teacher in Milton, Massachusetts. The students' solutions to the problem gave me a chance to assess their number sense and ability to reason numerically.

To prepare for the lesson, I purchased a 15-ounce box of raisins and a package of raisin mini-snacks. I showed them to the class and wrote the following information on the board:

14 raisin mini-snacks, $\frac{1}{2}$ ounce each	$1.49
1 box of raisins, 15 ounces	$1.89

"Which do you think is the better deal for the amount of money I spent?" I asked the class. I asked the students to talk about the problem at their tables. I find that having students talk in small groups gives more of them the chance to verbalize their ideas. Also, having the chance to talk before they write helps prepare them to put their ideas on paper.

After the students had talked among themselves for a few minutes, I called the class to attention and spent about 10 minutes having students report their ideas. Class discussions are useful for presenting students with different ways of approaching a problem. Hearing other points of view can provide students with options they might not have thought of themselves.

I then asked the students to write individual solutions to the problem. "Decide which is a better deal and explain your reasoning," I told them. "You're free to present any idea you wish, whether it was your idea or someone else thought of it, as long as you explain clearly why it makes sense."

"Can we work together?" Lindsey asked. Lindsey is a social child, always interested in interacting with others.

"You can talk with one another if it will help you clarify your thinking," I responded, "but you each are to write your own paper."

I wanted the students to have the freedom to talk with one another, as I've found that when they talk about their ideas, their writing is clearer and more complete. However, this time, I was interested in learning as much as possible about how each student would express his or her reasoning, so I decided that the students should write individually.

"Can I come up and look at the boxes?" Joel wanted to know.

"Yes," I said, "it's fine to refer to the boxes. Just leave them up here at the front of the room, so others can use them, too."

There were no other questions, and the students got to work. The students' papers and their methods of working revealed a variety of approaches. While some students mentally calculated that the entire package of mini-snacks weighed 7 ounces, others organized the mini-snacks into groups of two, either using the actual boxes or making sketches.

Some students calculated the price per ounce of each package. Melina, for example, included in her paper: *If you divide 14 into 1.49 you [get] about 10. So each little box is about 10 cents. If you divide 15 into 1.89 you get about 12. So each ½ oz is about 6 cents. The little boxes are 10¢ for ½! of a oz. The big box is obviously the better deal.*

The box is a better deal because if you double the weight (30 oz) the price would be about 3.78. If you double the weight (14 oz) it would be 2.98. If you divide 14 into 1.49 you about 10. So each little box is about 10 cents. If you divide 15 into 1.89 you get about 12. So each ½ oz is about 6 cents. The little boxes are 10¢ for ½! of a oz. The big box is drously the better deal. Plus the little boxes have to much uncassesory packaging, and plastic is hord to recycle and bad for the enviorment.

Melina's paper showed her concern for the environment. (Grade 5)

Some students compared two packages of mini-snacks to one box of raisins. James wrote: *I think that the 15 oz is a better deel because the 15 oz cost 1.89. But if you buy 2 of the ½ oz thats almost the same amount. (2.98 for 14 oz).*

Other students presented arguments without any numerical data. Gina wrote: *There are 7 oz. in the snack size and there are 15 oz. in the big box. 7 oz. is a little less than half of the big box and your getting twice as much without paying for twice as much. So clearly the big box is better!!!*

As students worked on their papers, I gave feedback and, at times, pushed for further information. Lindsey, for example, had written: *The 15 oz. box is the better deal because there are 7 oz.'s in the mini-snacks and there are 15 oz.'s in the big box. You get double the raisins for only 40¢ more.*

She felt she had completed the assignment, but I wasn't satisfied. "I don't think your argument is convincing," I said. "Suppose the big box cost 80 cents and the mini-snacks cost 40 cents. That would be double the price for double the raisins, and the cost would only be 40 cents more."

"I don't know what else to write," Lindsey said, discouraged. I suggested she talk it over with someone in her group. Soon she and Rachel were working together.

Lindsey added more to her paper to present a convincing argument. (Grade 5)

> **Math**
>
> The 15 oz. box is the better deal because there are 7 oz.s in the mini-snacks and there are 15 oz's in the big box. You get double the raisins for only 40¢ more. The big box is $1.89 and the little box is $1.49. You are saving $1.36 if you made the little box 15 oz.
>
> 7 oz. = $1.49
>
> 15 oz = $1.89
>
> There are 8 oz. separating the 7 oz from 15 oz. Each oz. is 22¢ in the little box.
>
> $$22¢ \times 8 \text{ oz.} = \$1.76$$
> $$1.49 + 1.76 = 3.25$$
>
> $ for 15 oz. in the little box. In the big box 15 oz. costs $1.89. The difference is $1.36, so you say $1.36.

The problem was too difficult for several students. For example, I read Annie's paper when she brought it to me. She had written: *The big box because you get more for your money and you get more raisins. In the other one you would get less raisins and less for your money.*

"Is there some way you can give a reason to convince someone why this is true?" I asked.

"What do you mean?" Annie asked.

"You tell me that the big box is a better buy, but you don't help me understand why," I said. "How about talking with someone else?"

"I'll talk with Joyce," Annie said.

When I read the papers that evening, I found that Annie had added a sentence: *Cause if you buy two packs of the mini-snacks you still don't get more oz.* Annie was right. Two packs of mini-snacks gave 14 ounces, which was still less than one 15-ounce box of raisins. Her explanation wasn't complete, but it was a good beginning.

Figuring out how to respond to students like Annie is one example of the kinds of instructional decisions teachers have to make daily. I try to find ways to probe and encourage without making students feel deficient. My decisions about interacting with students differ from child to child, based on what I know about the individual student's ability and interests. I know that Annie is a student who works slowly and has difficulty expressing her ideas, both orally and in writing, and I'm more gentle when I talk with her than I am with other students.

"Have you thought any more about the raisin problem?" I asked Annie the next day when she arrived in class. Annie shook her head no.

"I agree with what you added to your paper," I said. I showed Annie her paper. "If you buy two packs of the mini-snacks, you still don't get as much as you get with the big box." Annie nodded, seeming pleased, but also uneasy.

"You compared the amount of raisins, and I'm curious about how you would compare the amount of money you would spend in each case," I added.

"Is it right?" Annie asked.

"Yes," I responded, "what you wrote is correct, but I think more information is needed to make your argument convincing. Listen to other students' ideas when we talk about this today, and see if you get any ideas about how to talk about the difference in cost." Annie nodded.

Lyle also had difficulty with the problem. He wrote: *I think the big box is a better deal because one bag of mini snacks has 7 oz in it so you would have to buy 5 bags of the mini ones and have 5 little boxes left. But that would coust you 7.45. So its 4.30 more for 5 more oz.*

> I can prove that the Sun Maid Raisins are a better deal than the mini packs.
>
> If the mini packs are 7oz. altoghether, and the Sun Maid pack is 15 oz. well you basically get a better deal.
>
> Here is one way to prove Sun Maid is a better deal.
>
> mini packs
>
> $149   7oz.
> $2.98   14oz.
> $4.47   21oz.
>
> Sun Maid
>
> $1.89   15oz.
> $3.78   30oz.
>
> You can get 21 oz. of mini packs for $4.47. And you can get 30oz. of Sun Maid for $3.78.
> I have proved my case.

Zev compared the prices of different quantities of raisins. (Grade 5)

I hadn't had a chance to talk with Lyle during class, but I had noticed that he was busy working on his paper. I had taught Lyle when he was in third grade, so I knew that he had put enormous effort into this paper. After thinking about what he wrote, I thought I understood how he had reasoned. Buying five bags of mini-snacks would give 35 ounces of raisins and cost $7.45. Buying two of the 15-ounce boxes would also give 30 ounces. But the $4.30 didn't make sense. Since two 15-ounce boxes cost $3.78, it would be $3.67 more, not $4.30 more. Also, the extra 5 ounces would mean 10 little boxes, not 5 little boxes as Lyle said.

Although Lyle's paper was flawed in several ways, I knew it represented a great deal of growth for him. I tried talking with him the next day, but he wasn't able to reconstruct his thinking. "Was I wrong?" he asked. I saw a familiar look flash across his face, almost a kind of despair.

"I don't think your reasoning was wrong," I said, "but I think there's something goofy about the numbers. I spent about 10 minutes or so last night thinking about your paper. Let me see if I understood what you were thinking."

The time I spent with Lyle was important. It gave me a chance to encourage him to continue taking risks in his thinking as well as to give him feedback about his work. I'm always aware of how hard it is to balance encouraging and questioning a student, especially when that student has a shaky self-concept.

Also on the next day, the class discussed the different solutions. Students volunteered to present their work, and others asked questions and evaluated whether their own approaches were similar or different. Annie remained quiet during the discussion, but I could tell that she was paying attention. I pointed out to the class that it was difficult for some students to follow others' reasoning. "That's why it's important to figure things out for yourself," I said.

This was also a good reminder for me that my teaching explanations are only valuable when students can reconstruct the thinking for themselves.

Using Percents (Grades 7 and 8)

Cathy Humphreys's seventh and eighth graders in San Jose, California, were learning about percents. Partway through the unit, Cathy assessed their ability to use percents in a problem-solving situation. She posed a problem created by Lynne Alper, a math educator with the EQUALS program at the Lawrence Hall of Science in Berkeley, California. Cathy wrote on the board:

> A school has 500 students. If a school bus holds 75 students, is there enough room on one bus for all the school's left-handed students?

Cathy first had the students report on a class graph whether they were right-handed or left-handed. They analyzed the data and compared them to the information Cathy had researched that 12 percent to $12\frac{1}{2}$ percent of Americans are left-handed. The students then tackled the problem, working in pairs. Listening as partners discussed the problem provided Cathy with some information about the students' perceptions. Reading the students' solutions contributed further to Cathy's assessment of their understanding and confusion.

Several pairs of students multiplied to solve the problem. Liz and Audrey wrote: *To get the answer we multiplied 500 students by 12% and got 60 people and the bus can hold 75 people so there is enough room.*

Joey and Tony multiplied 12.5×5 and got 62.5. They rounded this up to 63 and wrote: *Yes, because there are 63 students that are left handed.*

Other students used different reasoning processes. Marshay and Kiet wrote: *Yes, there are enough seats to hold all of the left handed people because 10% of 500 is 50 people, 2% of 500 is 10 people, so 50 + 10 is 60 people, and each bus holds 75 people.*

Eric and James wrote: *Yes, there are enough seats on the bus to fit the left-handed children. There are 63 left handed kids. We got the answer by using part of our homework. 10% of 500 is 50. 5% of 500 is 25—this was halved.*

Khalil and Gina took a different approach: *We think you can because 75 is 15% of 500. We only have to put 12% on of the left handed people.*

Right answers alone can hide a lack of understanding. No matter the method they chose, all of the students arrived at the correct answer that there was enough room for all the left-handed students. If the students had only reported answers, Cathy might not have learned about some of the students' confusion. Their written responses served to alert Cathy to some conceptual misunderstandings.

For example, some groups tried using division. Jon and Phi, for example, divided 12 into 500 and wrote: *After we did the problem we got 41.66 and it kept on going on so we rounded it off to 42 students. We then subtracted 75 into 42 and got 33. After we got 33 seats we knew all the left handed people could get on the bus.*

Raymond, Paula, and Stephanie also used division, but they divided 500 into 12. They wrote: *Yes, 12 ÷ 500 = 0.024 (12% ÷ 500 students) so out of 500 students 24 of them are left handed so the bus can hold all the left handed people.*

Raymond, Paula, and Stephanie came to the right conclusion, but their paper revealed their lack of understanding. (Grade 8)

Table 5

Yes, there are enough seats to hold all of the left-handed people because 10% of 500 is 50 people, 2% of 500 is 10 people, so 50 + 10 is 60 people and each bus holds 75 people.

School Bus Problem

We think you can because 75 is 15% of 500. We only have to put 12% on of the left handed people.

School Bus Problem

There will be 60 left-handed students on the bus.

Out of 100 12% would be 12 people. since 500 is 5x more than 100 you times

12 × 5 = 60.

Each of these papers showed a different way to explain why there was room on the bus for all of the left-handed students. (Grade 8)

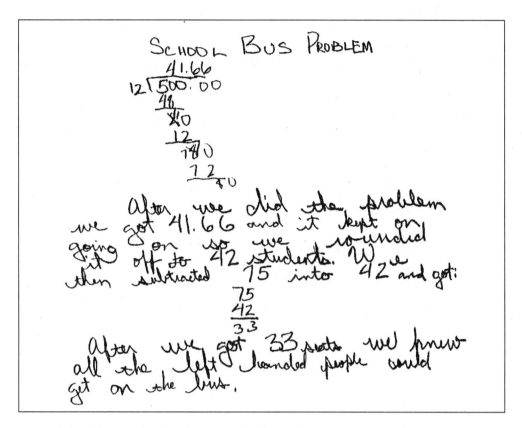

Jon and Phi did not understand how to solve the problem. (Grade 8)

Cathy followed this assessment with an individual writing assignment titled: "What I Know About Percents (So Far)." She told the students that their writing would help her to learn what they understood and therefore help her plan more effectively for their continued learning. A writing assignment such as this gives value to students' thoughts and involves students in reflecting on their own learning processes.

"How much do we have to write?" Raymond asked.

"What I'm interested in," Cathy responded, "is getting as complete a picture as possible of what you understand. I imagine that will take a full page, more or less. What's important is that you include as many details as possible."

"Should we tell how we solve problems?" Nam asked.

"If that will give me information about your thinking and understanding, then it would be helpful," Cathy answered. "The more information you provide, the better."

In their papers, the students included information about what percents are, situations in which percents are used, and ways to represent percents. Darshana, for example, wrote: *I know that percent is used for many things.*

It is used for grading, weather, tiping, and survaying. I learned how to Estamate more accurtly. I also learned that 100 is the main factor in percents. That means a pie is 100% or, 2% means .02 hundredths. Fractions are related to percents. That means ½ is also 50%. Some good [ways] to figure out percents are pencil and paper, calculator, and your mind.

Darshana gave examples of how percents are used. (Grade 8)

> What I know about Percent (so far)
>
> I know that percent is used for many things. It is used for grading, weather, tiping, and survayig. I learn how to Estamate more accuretly. I also learned that 100 is the main factor in percents. That means a pie is 100% or, 2% mean .02 hundredths. Fractions are related to percents. That means ½ is also 50%. Somegood to figure out percents are pencil and paper, calculator, and your mind.
>
> We also learn people use chartes to figure out percents like this:
>
> 50% of 600 is 300
>
> 25% of 600 is 150
> et.
> et
> etc.

Dwight wrote: *I know that percent has to do with decimals. You can make a decimal into a percentage. Percent is used in odds, for example 60% rain and 20% humidity. Percents are used every day in the United*

States. When sports announcers announce sports they see what team has a better percentage of winning the game. Percentage also has to do with 100. I think the term "percent" is an easier way of figuring out a problem.* Dwight gave his paper an A+.

Some students also included ways of calculating. For example, Eric wrote: *I know that percent is a type of ratio. Percent is used to figure out how many out of one-hundred something is. Like what percent of a hundred apples are green or yellow or red.*

People use percent in all sorts of ways. Such as figuring out budgets for vacations, the chance of rain, and how much of what is in the air.

Percentage is used for many other things in our world too. Percent is a simple, accurate way to figure things out.

Here is a table to help with percent

50%	of	500	is	250
25%	of	500	is	125
10%	of	500	is	50
5%	of	500	is	25
1%	of	500	is	5

Eric made a chart "to help with percent." (Grade 7)

Lemuel wrote: *What I know is that it has to do with 100 and if you want to find out something like what is 1% of $500 you could use a calculator to multiply $500 by .01 which equals to $5.00 or if it's easy enough to do in your head you don't need to use a calculator. You can also use percent to find out how many students in this school are right handers and how many are left handers, etc.*

Heather wrote: *What I know about percent so far is that you use it when you are tipping a waitress, figuring out a sale and weather forecasting. I know that 50% of something is half and 25% of something is one fourth. Percents can be changed from fractions. Also if 60% of rain is predicted one day and 40% the next I know that doesn't mean a 100% chance of rain. And if you get a 90% on a test it means you're doing real well and got an A–. I also know that in order to find 20% of a $34.00 top you must divide $34.00 by five because 5 times 20% equals 100%. So 20% of $34.00 is $6.80.*

An issue that appeared in several students' papers was how large percents can be. Nam, for example, began his paper with: *I know that the maximum percent is 100.* Jena, however, began her paper with: *I know that if there were 100 dollars each would count for 1%. Percent can go up to 100%, and sometimes over.* Nin wrote: *Parts of a whole have to sum up to 100%. The percent of a whole is 100%. Doubling will be 100% more. Tripling will be 200% more and so on.* Tony wrote: *I know that percent is what a number is out of 100. There is no percent higher than 100%.*

Some students wrote about difficulties they were having. Tony also included in his paper: *I know that $25 is twenty-five percent out of $100. I know that $\frac{1}{5}$ is 20% out of 100%. I also know that percents are used everywhere and alot of the time. Some problems that I have with percents are the ones I don't understand. For example 13% out of $15.00. Or 23 percent out of $300.00. These problems and some problems like these are the ones I don't really understand. I guess the ones I don't understand are the ones that have an odd number for a percent.*

Jon wrote: *The first thing I think about when I hear percent is 100%. I know that most of the time when you want to find how percent of something is you usually use 100%. I also know that there are many ways to get answers and that is when I get confused. Sometimes I know how to do it and sometimes I don't. Percent to me is a guess or an estimate and later you try to find the real percent. I think percent is kind of easy and hard.*

Stephanie wrote about her confusion: *So far all I know about percent is that it is very confusing! I think I understand how to solve a percent problem but since we didn't do percents last year this is my first time doing percents I am easily confused when a new way to solve a problem pops out* at me. Here is an example of what I think when you ask what 20% means to me. Well if you take a dollar you know that there are 100 pennies in that dollar. And when you have that 100% that means that each penny stands for 1% so 20% of a dollar is 20 cents.

> What I Know About
> Percent (so far)
>
> I know that percent is a part of something. I also know that percent uses a sign like this: %. Also percent is something out of 100, like 50% of 100 would be 50 because 50% is like ½ of 100. Percent is used with big numbers and when surveys are taken. People used percent to determine how much of something. (ex) 5% of 500 people = 100 people.) I know how to work with percent, but it is hard to explain what I know about it. All I know is that I can use percent to help me.

Phi had some ideas about how percent is used but found it hard to explain what he knew. (Grade 8)

From reading the students' papers, Cathy learned about the range of their understanding and their levels of confidence. The papers also provided some specific direction for further instruction. The references to the possible maximum size of percents were an indication that this issue needed attention in class. Also, the frequent mention of money was evidence of its usefulness for helping students think about percents.

Part 2

TYPES OF WRITING ASSIGNMENTS

Over the years since I began using writing in the math class, four categories of writing assignments evolved—keeping journals or logs, solving math problems, explaining mathematical ideas, and writing about thinking processes. Each category focuses students on different aspects of their learning and provides different ways for teachers to assess what students are actually doing and learning.

I've found that individual students tend to enjoy one kind of writing assignment more than another. Also, I've found that different classes respond in general more positively to some types of assignments than to others. I've tried analyzing students' responses to find out, for example, if preferences differ for older or younger students, or for more or less capable math students. However, I've never seen any patterns of evidence that satisfy me as conclusive. With each class, I learn about students' mathematical interests and abilities and create assignments to help them learn to express their mathematical thinking in writing.

Keeping Journals or Logs

Journals or logs are a way for students to keep ongoing records about what they're doing and learning in math class. Reading students' writing for any particular day gives me a general overview of the responses from a class, as well as insights into the different ideas individual students understand, enjoy, or think are important.

I spend time, especially at the beginning of the school year, discussing with students what they are to write in their journals. I generally give students three guidelines:

- Write about what you did.
- Write about what you learned.
- Write about what you're not sure about or wondering about.

I post these guidelines so they're available for the students to review, and I reinforce them on a regular basis. Also, I remind students from time to time that their writing is important, as it contributes to the planning I do for my teaching.

When students are beginning to write in journals or logs, I sometimes post prompts for them to use as suggestions:

Today I _____.
I learned _____.
I'm not sure about _____.
I'm wondering about _____.

On some days, depending on what we did in class, I give students specific guidelines for journal entries. For example, I might say, "Write about what was easy and what was difficult for you in solving this problem." I might give a direction such as, "Explain why Elly's answer made sense," or "Write about why Marina and Josh disagreed." I might ask students to write about a particular activity, or I might give them several suggestions from which to choose.

Over the years, I've changed the ways I've organized journal writing, and I've found benefits and limitations in each of my systems. Sometimes I've stapled sheets of paper into booklets with construction paper covers and given students new booklets for each unit. A benefit of this system is that students get a fresh start, which they seem to enjoy, each time we begin a new unit. A disadvantage is that I have to lug home a class set of booklets to read their work.

Sometimes I've had students write on separate sheets of paper each day and hand them in; after I read them, I file them in their folders. This system makes it easier for me to read a class set without carrying home a pile of booklets and then rummaging through each one to find the current entry. However, when reading students' papers at home, I can't check back on any previous work until I return to school.

One year, when teaching middle school students, I gave each student a spiral-bound notebook of paper ruled into $\frac{1}{4}$-inch squares. This method had the benefit of allowing them to graph with ease, but it was an expensive investment.

I've kept one consistent policy, however, which I made after too many students didn't bring their journals to school or, even worse, lost them: Students' journals or logs stay in the classroom, except when I take them home to read.

I've also changed how often I have students write in their journals. In some instances, I've made time for students to write every day. I do this especially at the beginning of the year when I'm helping students become accustomed to writing in math class. Also, it's useful to have students write daily when studying something new so that they can reflect regularly on their thinking. At other times, I have students write an average of once or twice a week, depending on what other sort of writing we're doing. Sometimes, I don't have students keep a journal or log for a unit, especially when I know they'll be doing a good deal of writing for assignments throughout the unit.

Probability (Grade 3)

During a unit on probability that I was teaching to a class of third graders, I introduced an activity called *Spinner Sums.* The activity called for spinning two spinners, adding the numbers they landed on, and recording the sums to see what sums came up most often. There were two different spinners to choose from, giving three possible pairings of spinners for the activity.

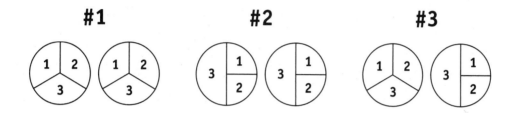

Because each spinner had the numbers 1, 2, and 3 on it, there were five possible sums—2, 3, 4, 5, and 6. The recording sheet for the activity had five columns, one for each sum. The students spun the spinners and recorded each sum in the proper column. When a column was filled, that sum "won." So that we could look at a larger sample of data, I posted a class chart on which children were to record the sums that "won" for each of the three versions.

In an earlier class discussion, we had analyzed the possible ways to get each sum. To get a 2, for example, the children had to spin a 1 on each spinner; to get a 3, they needed to spin 1 on the first spinner and 2 on the second, or 2 on the first and 1 on the second. On the board, I listed the possible ways to make each sum:

2	3	4	5	6
1 + 1	1 + 2	1 + 3	2 + 3	3 + 3
	2 + 1	3 + 1	3 + 2	
		2 + 2		

Before the students began to play the game, I asked the class a question. "What sum do you think is most likely to win?" I purposely didn't specify which two spinners I was thinking of, but was interested in what the students thought in general. Several had comments.

"The 4 should win," Emelia said.

"That's what I was going to say," Doug said.

"Me, too," several others added.

"But it doesn't make sense to me that you'd get the same results from each version," I said.

"That's what I was thinking," Abby said. "I think that the ones with the big space for 3 would make 6 win." The others were impressed with Abby's observation and most agreed.

"What about the pair with two different spinners?" I asked, pointing to version 3.

"It's got to be different, too," Andrew said. "Maybe 5 will win with them." Others thought that was a good idea.

"We'll think more about this later," I said, "after you've had time to try the experiments and report data for each of the three versions."

I circulated to observe the students. Amanda stopped me and showed me her recording sheet for the first version. She said, "Look, mine worked perfectly!"

"What do you mean by perfectly?" I asked.

"Well, 4 won," she said, "just like on the chart."

"The chart also shows that 2 and 6 can come up the same number of ways," I said. "But you got 6 more times."

"But it's pretty perfect," she said.

"When you write today, be sure to describe what happened when you played the game and what surprised you," I said. Amanda nodded, and got up to record on the class chart.

Spinner Sums #3

Today, I played Spinner Sums #3 I had the 1 spinner and the second spinner. I spun a 2 and a 3 on my first roll, I got a lot of 2 and 3. at first I thought 5 would win but 5 didint 4 did, I was suprised that dubl ones came up 4 times and doble 3's came up 5 times in order of how came up to the top first gose like this 4, 3, 5, 6, 2. I was suprised that 4 had 3 dabl 2's not just all 3 and 1's. I conted all the doubles and all the dabls of 4, 2 and 6 are 12 dobls, I relley thought that 5 would win and even be a hed of 3.

Spinner Sums #1

		3+1		
		1+3		
		2+2		
		3+1		
		1+3		
		3+1		
	2+1	1+3		
	1+2	2+2	2+3	
	2+1	3+1	3+2	
	1+2	2+2	2+3	
	2+1	1+3	3+2	3+3
	1+2	3+1	2+3	3+3
	2+1	1+3	3+2	3+3
1+1	1+2	3+1	2+3	3+3
2	3	4	5	6

Amanda wrote about what happened and what surprised her about her results from Spinner Sums. (Grade 3)

When students notice something, make an observation, or report a discovery that I think is mathematically interesting, I encourage them to write about the idea in their journals. This sort of encouragement not only gives students the message that I value their ideas but also helps me remember what they were thinking when I read their writing later.

Erin brought three recording sheets to me. "This is crazy," she said.

"What's crazy?" I asked.

"I used spinners with the big space for 3, and 4 won three times," Erin said. "Look!"

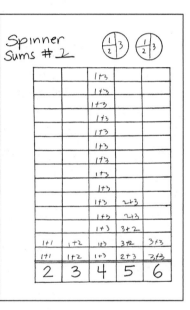

Erin's recording sheets gave results that surprised her. (Grade 3)

"What did you think would happen?" I asked.

"I thought 6 should win, like Abby said," Erin answered. "But it didn't. Maybe it's just chance, but it's goofy." She went over to show her results to Abby.

Charlie and Alan came up to me. Charlie looked perplexed, but Alan was laughing. "What's up?" I said.

"He's upset," Alan said, nodding his head at Charlie. "He was sure that 5 would win, but it didn't even come out close." Charlie showed me his paper. He had done version 3 with one of each spinner; 4 had won and 5 had come up only once.

"It just doesn't make sense," Charlie said, shaking his head.

The activity was one of several that children could choose during math time, and after about a week, a good deal of data were posted on the class chart. I called the children's attention to the data and asked what they noticed.

"The 2s and 3s hardly won at all," Emelia said. "That was just what I suspected."

"The 2s did worst of all," Elliot added.

"I think it's weird how the 4s did the best on all of them," Seth said.

"Maybe we didn't do it enough times," Lee Ann said.

"The 6 didn't do so good," Alan said.

"It won for me," Abby said.

"But not a lot for the whole class," Kristin said.

"It did okay on version 2," Ajani pointed out.

"When I did it, I got a lot of double 1s and 3s," Amanda said. "It was very surprising."

"That's not about the chart," Lori chided her.

"I know," Amanda responded breezily, "but it happened."

"I think it's all chance," Lisa said. "You really can't tell what will happen. It depends how you spin. If you spin hard, you can get different things than if you spin easy."

"You're supposed to spin hard," Charlie said. "You're not supposed to try and get some number. It's not fair then."

"But it's still chance," Lisa insisted.

"I have an idea," Andrew said. "I think that the middle number still has power, even though the spinners look different."

"But 6 got more on version 2 with the bigger space for 3," Abby answered, "so the spinners do count."

Andrew said, "I played with Eric. We did 10 games and 6 won five times, but 4 won four times. I didn't think 4 would win that much. And 5 only won 1 time."

Charlie had a different view. "But 6 only has one way of coming up, with 3 and 3."

"But 3 has half of the spinner," Erin said.

"But the 3 can make a 4, too, not just a 6," Charlie countered.

"I'm still confused," Erin added.

Although the students had chosen different activities to do during class that day, I asked them all to write about Spinner Sums in their journals. "Include your ideas about what happened when you played, what you expected to come up, and what you learned about the probability of the sums," I told them. "You may want to include an idea you expressed in the discussion, or an idea you learned from someone else."

The students' responses revealed to me their different interpretations of the mathematics and reactions to their experiences with Spinner Sums. For example, Abby explained her theory that 6 should win. She wrote: *Today I played Spinner Sums 2. It came out how I expected, six won. I expected this because three had as much space in the spinner as two and one put together. I expected that both of the spinners whould spin three a lot and that would make six so six whould win.* She went on to explain why she thought 4 and 5 were equally likely.

> Today I played Spinner Sums 2. It came out how I expected, six won. I expected this because three had as much space in the spinner as two and one put together. I expected that both of the spinners whould spin three a lot and that would make six so six whould win. I think four and five should be equally likely to come up because two and one have the same chance of coming up and they both have a three in it. But in four I could have gotton two and two but I did not that seemed unlikely to me. Also three and two

Abby explained why she thought that 6 had the best chance of winning. (Grade 3)

> have somthing weird about them, three has three more than two and two and three are equally likely because one and two are equally likely on the spinner and one and two have the same chance of coming up and so dose one and one.

Charlie wrote at length about why he felt that 4 was most likely to come up. It took him several pages to explain his thinking, and although his language was imprecise, his thinking was impressive.

Something interesting is even though 6 has only one possibility it has a three in it. And on the spinner three has the biggest space which could let six do a lot better because the only possibility for six is 3+3! It seems that numbers that don't have three in one or more possibilitys don't do as well because of the spinner. 1 and 2 only have 25% each and the

only combonations for three are 1+2 and 2+1 three barely comes up at all. Also 2's only combonation is 1+1 which gives it almost no hope of coming up. One of my other experiments was to see the best number in coming up. 4 seems to come up a lot because it has three combonations. 2+2, 3+1 and 1+3. Since four has a three it is increased in coming up and

it has the most combonations of all the numbers. Then I decided to see the second best number. It turned out to be five. It was not a big surprise seeing five has 3 in two of its combonations and has 2 combonations. You probably are thinking "Why not three coming up second?" but remember three doesn't have a three in one of its combonations

Charlie wrote at length about why 4 was the most likely sum to come up. (Grade 3)

There's typically a difference in what students write about, how much they write, and how they express themselves. Not all students are interested in or capable of focusing on the mathematics. Janos's writing, for example, indicated that he hadn't had a very good day. He wrote: *All I learnd is it takes too long and jivan cheats, and It's not fair! and who ever gets to the finish line first wins.*

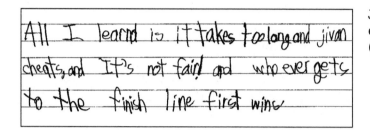

Janos wasn't pleased with his experience during class. (Grade 3)

Fractions (Grade 4)

On the fifth day of fraction instruction, to assess the students' understanding, I asked them to write in their journals about whether ½ or ⅓ was larger and to explain why.

Lydia's journal entry showed she understood the importance of identifying the whole when interpreting fractions. (Grade 4)

Darius brought his journal to me to read. He had written: *One thered is like a quorter One half is like two quarters and two quarters is more then one quarters so two quorters is more.* I talked with Darius about why a third and a quarter were different, but I wasn't able to make much headway convincing him.

"Maybe other students can help explain," I said. "How would you feel about continuing our discussion with the rest of the class?"

"Okay," Darius said, "I can read what I wrote." Darius is a confident and well-liked child. He had no qualms about exposing his ideas to the scrutiny of his classmates. (If Darius were at all timid about making his ideas public, I would not have asked.)

Darius's paper sparked a lively class discussion. (Grade 4)

One thered is like a quorter
One half is like Two
quorters and two quorters
is more then One quorters
So Two quorters is more.

The next day, I began class by telling the students about my difficulty convincing Darius why I thought what he had written was incorrect. Darius read his paper aloud. I asked the children to talk with their neighbors about what Darius had written, and then I began a class discussion.

First, I had Darius come to the front of the room to explain his reasoning. He took a yellow hexagon from the Pattern Blocks and arranged three blue parallelograms on it. "The yellow hexagon is a whole," he said, "and you can fit three quarters on it. And a half is bigger than one of them."

Students made different arguments to Darius about his reasoning. Mia said, "It takes four quarters to make a dollar. If you have three quarters, then you only have 75 cents. And you need 100 cents to make a whole dollar, so you can't call them quarters."

Gavin said, "They're not quarters. There are only three of them, so they're thirds. You have to call them thirds."

Teddy said, "If you call them quarters, then you have to have four of them, and that would mean one extra outside of the hexagon."

Carly said, "One third isn't a quarter. It's bigger than a quarter. They're not the same."

To each argument, Darius insisted that he knew that he needed four quarters to make a whole. "At least usually," he said, "but in this instance, you can only fit three blocks on the whole, so three quarters make a whole." Nothing anyone said changed his mind.

I wasn't clear about whether Darius's misconception was based on confusion over the language or over the concept, but it was early in the unit, and I've come to expect that when students learn something new, their understanding typically is partial, and confusion often exists.

> 1/2 is larger than 1/3. 1/2 in a hexagon is a rhombus and a triangle. 1/3 is only a rhombus. 1/2 is 2 quarters. 1/3 is 1 quarter. In fractions the lower number is larger I think that 1/2 is bigger because I did it in my head and I used pattern blocks. Picture ↓
>
> 
>

Justin showed what he knew and what he was still confused about. (Grade 4)

> Which is larger – $\frac{1}{2}$ or $\frac{1}{3}$? Explain Why.
>
> $\frac{1}{2}$ is larger. It is larger because $\frac{1}{3}$ has 3 pieses to make a whole. The more pieses there is, the smaller they are. So one half is 2 pieses and you only dived it into two and the peises are bigger

Michelle's journal entry showed her understanding of fractional notation. (Grade 4)

It was then time for recess. When the class returned, I shifted gears and taught them how to play Wipeout, a game using Pattern Blocks and fraction dice numbered with $\frac{1}{2}$, $\frac{1}{3}$, $\frac{1}{3}$, $\frac{1}{6}$, $\frac{1}{6}$, $\frac{1}{6}$. Students played in twos or threes. To play, each player started with three yellow hexagons, each of which was considered one whole. The goal was to be the first player to get rid of the blocks. Each student took a turn rolling a die. On a turn, a player was allowed to exchange a block for an equivalent amount of other Pattern Blocks, remove a block the value of the fraction that came up on the die, or do nothing.

Several days earlier, I had taught the children the game of Cover Up, using strips of different colors of construction paper cut into halves, fourths, eighths, and sixteenths and different fraction dice with $\frac{1}{2}$, $\frac{1}{4}$, $\frac{1}{8}$, $\frac{1}{8}$, $\frac{1}{16}$, and $\frac{1}{16}$ on them. In that game, the students had to cover up their whole strip of paper. As each player rolled a die, he or she used an equivalent strip of paper to cover up part of the whole strip. Both games gave the children experience linking the symbolism of fractions to concrete materials. Wipeout also involved the students with exchanging quantities for equivalent amounts.

I let the students play Wipeout for about 20 minutes and then asked them to put away the blocks and come to attention. I led a discussion in which I asked the students what they liked about the game. Several students said that Wipeout was a better game than Cover Up.

I then asked what strategies they had used for playing. Nick presented the strategy he had used for exchanging blocks. "I exchanged the yellow hexagon for one red, one blue, and one green," he said. "That way, I was sure to be able to take something off on my next turn."

Lindsey had a different approach. "I think it's better to exchange the hexagon for two blues and two greens, like making a peace sign," she said. "You don't roll $\frac{1}{2}$ very much." Lindsey showed with Pattern Blocks what she meant.

These two points of view sparked a good deal of interest, and there was a lively interchange. Finally, I brought the discussion to a close to leave time for the students to write in their journals. On the board I wrote suggestions for what they could write:

My strategy for Wipeout is _____.
What I think about Lindsey's and Nick's ideas is _____.
I like Wipeout better than Cover Up because _____.
What I did today was _____.
What I'd like to say to Darius is _____.

"Here are five ideas about what you might write about today," I said. "If you're not sure what you want to write, or if you don't know how to begin, read these over and choose one to help you get started. You don't have to use any of these ideas, but they're suggestions that you can use if you'd like."

Almost half of the students wrote about their strategies for playing Wipeout. I think that the discussion about Nick's and Lindsey's strategies was the impetus for most of these papers. Cori, for example, wrote: *My strategy for wipe out is that if I wanted to excange a full half of a hexagone, I would exchange it for a rhonbus and a triangle. Because you more likely to roll a $\frac{1}{6}$ which is a triagle or a $\frac{1}{3}$ which is a rhonbus then a $\frac{1}{2}$ which is the half of a hexagone.*

Cori's journal entry focused on her strategy for Wipeout. (Grade 4)

Gavin wrote: *My strategy for Wipe out is that if you exchange a yellow for a red, blue, and green you have a 100% chance that you'll get to put one in the bucket. But with the peace sign you only have a 75% chance to put one in the bucket.*

I talked with Gavin about how he arrived at the 75 percent chance. He responded, "I knew it was more than 50 percent because there's only one chance that you would roll a $\frac{1}{2}$, and it seemed like more than 60 percent, too, so I said 75 percent."

Four students wrote both about their strategies for Wipeout and why they liked it better than Cover Up. Teddy, for example, wrote: *I like wipe-out more than cover-up Because well I think that it is more fun it is more suspencful and it has more strategy in it. I think the best strategy for wipe-out is to do 4 triangles and one diamond then the next time you exchange you should take 1 half 1 triangle and 1 diamond. When I was playing Wipeout I was always using 1 diamond 1 half and 1 triangle and I lost almost every time. I think this game is some chance some strategy because rolling the dice is chance exchanging is strategy.*

Five children wrote only about why they liked Wipeout better than Cover Up. Andrea, for example, wrote: *I [like] Wipeout better than coverup. Wipeout has more action. You get to use pattern blocks wich I like. And your not just useing little peces of paper. And in Whipout your useing your BRAIN, because you need to know wich fraction is wich peice. And in cover up you dont need your brain cause everything has a label on it.*

In her journal entry, Andrea explained why she liked Wipeout better than Cover Up. (Grade 4)

> I Wipeout better than cover up. Wipeout has more action. You get to use pattern blocks wich I like. And your not just useing little peices of paper. And in whipout your useing your BRAIN. because you need to know wich fraction is wich peice. And in cover up you dont need your brain cause everything has a label on it.

Katy and Madeleine wrote letters to Darius. Katy wrote: *Dear Darius, I did not get why you comparing ¼'s with ⅓'s & ½'s. I don't agree with you about ⅓ is like ¼ because I know that they are both totally different fractions. I do agree with you about ½ being like ²⁄₄'s because I know that is true because if you add ¼ + ¼ you wil get ½. Darius I think some other day you will have to explain your thing with the ⅓'s.*

Katy wrote a letter to Darius explaining why she disagreed with him. (Grade 4)

> Dear Darius,
> I did not get why your comparing ¼'s with ⅓'s & ½'s. I dont agree with you about ⅓ is like ¼ because I know that they are both totally different fractions. I do agree with you about ½ being like ²⁄₄'s because I know that is true because if you add ¼ + ¼ you will get ½. Darius I think some other day you will have to explain your thing with the ⅓'s.

Justin wrote about Darius's thinking and also included his thoughts about his strategy for Wipeout: *What I think about Darius is that in a fantasy world there would be 75¢ for a dollar, so in that case ⅓ would be a quarter. But, if you tried to make 4 ⅓ in a hexagon it wouldn't work.*

My strategy for wipeout is the peace sign and six triangles. Usually I get ⅙'s, but sometimes I get ⅓'s, so the peace sign is good. Sometimes I get all ⅙'s so that is good too.

What I think about Darius is that in a fantasy world there would be 75¢ for a dollar, so in that case 1/3 would be a quarter. But, if you tried to make 4 1/3 in a hexagon it wouldn't work.

My strategy for wipeout is the peace sign and six triangles. Usually I get 1/6's, but sometimes I get 1/3's, so the peace sign is good. Sometimes I get all 1/6's so that is good too.

Justin responded to Darius and also wrote about his strategy for Wipeout. (Grade 4)

Molly brought her own style to her writing. She wrote: *I really thought that this was much more fun than Cover up becauase it is more exiting than cover up. I also thought that wipeout was much better because you had decisions and you don't just roll the dice and roll the dice and roll the dice!*

I think that what Darius said was a little bit wacko and I did not quite understand it.

Roll Two Dice (Grade 2)

In one of the second grade classes I taught, I found that the children had great difficulty writing about their experiences in math class. To focus them on what to write, I had them brainstorm words they could use to begin their writing. "For example," I said, "you could start a sentence with 'I noticed' or 'I learned.'" I wrote these phrases on a sheet of chart paper that I had posted.

"Does anyone have another idea about how to start writing?" I asked.

The children had several suggestions. "I saw." "I predicted." "I thought."

I added their suggestions to the chart paper. Also, I prepared half-sheets for their writing and had a supply available for them to use. I encouraged the children to take a sheet whenever they had an idea they wanted to write down, not just to wait for me to ask them to write. The small paper size seemed to be manageable for the children, and involving them in thinking about how to begin writing helped them understand the assignment.

I didn't ask the children to write every day, but chose days when I had introduced something new or when they were particularly involved with activities. For example, I taught the children *Roll Two Dice,* an activity that engaged them in practicing basic addition facts and thinking about the probabilities of the different sums. I gave the children squared paper and showed them how to write the numbers from 2 to 12 across the bottom and record each combination they rolled in the correct column until one sum reached the top.

The sum of 8 "won" in this game of Roll Two Dice. (Grade 2)

The children's writing described their different experiences. Some described what happened. Catherine, for example, wrote: *Today I played Roll 2 Dice 2 times. I Noticed that 8 won 2 times.*

Others wrote about what they had learned. Sophia, for example, wrote: *Today I played Roll two dice. I learned that you can get the number 7 alot. I did not get enough time to finish it. It is just chance.*

Name: Michael
Date: 2-3-93
Today I played Roll 2 Dice and 9 won. I predicted it would win. I like it. by the way the game I played is just chance because you roll 2 Dice.

Name: Catherine
Date: 2,3, 1993
Today I Played Roll 2 Dice 2 times
I Noticed that 8 won 2 times

Name: David
Date: 2-3-1993
Today I learned that you have to go up to 12 in Roll 2 Dice

Name: Sophia
Date: 2-3-92
Today I played Roll two dice.
I learned that you can get the number 7 a lot. I did not get enough time to finish it. It is just chance.

These children wrote about their experiences playing Roll Two Dice. (Grade 2)

Solving Math Problems

The NCTM *Standards* states: "Problem solving is the process by which students experience the power and usefulness of mathematics in the world around them" (page 75). In their school learning, students need a great deal of experience applying mathematical skills to problem situations. Classroom lessons should help students learn to use a variety of strategies to solve problems, to verify and interpret results, and to generalize solutions to new problem situations. Writing requires students to formulate and clarify their ideas and, therefore, can contribute to helping students develop these abilities.

When solving problems, students should be required not only to present answers but also to explain their reasoning. I tell children that their papers should convince the reader that their solutions are correct and also reveal how the students arrived at their solutions.

When students solve problems in class, I encourage them to bring their papers to me as they finish, and I often read and discuss their papers with them. I question their thinking, challenge weak arguments, and push them to include more details. If I don't have time to talk with them, I may write notes on their papers asking them to address my questions or concerns. At all times, I keep the emphasis on their thinking and reasoning.

The Paint Problem (Grade 5)

After talking with a class of fifth graders about how mixing red paint and yellow paint produces orange paint, I posed a problem to see which students would be able to reason proportionally. "Suppose I made one batch of paint by mixing two parts of red paint and two parts of yellow," I said, "and another batch by mixing three parts of red paint and two parts of yellow. How would the colors compare?" I wrote on the board:

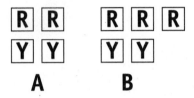

It was obvious to the students that B would be a darker color. Their responses indicated that they understood that more yellow paint would produce a lighter orange and more red would produce a darker orange.

I then asked the students to compare the colors of two other samples. I wrote on the board:

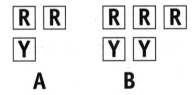

As I often do before asking students to write solutions to problems, I had them discuss their ideas. Some students argued that the two samples would be the same color.

"They both have more red," Matt stated, "so they'll both be dark orange."

"There's more paint in B," Amy said, "but they'll both be the same color."

Other students disagreed. "There's twice as much red as yellow in A, but only a little more red in B," Andy said.

"B would be darker because it has more red," Sol said.

"It doesn't matter that B has more red," Theresa argued. "B has more yellow, too."

"Look," Victoria said in an exasperated tone, "you'd have to have another part of red in B for them to be the same."

After the discussion had gone back and forth, I posed the problem again, asking the students to write about their ideas. "Record what you think about how the colors compare," I said, "and explain your thinking."

As I circulated and read the students' papers, I made notes on some of them to probe those students' thinking. In a way, I was having dialogues in writing with the students. I initiate dialogues like these for various reasons. Sometimes I'm not quite sure what a student is thinking and I want additional information. Sometimes a student seems particularly eager, so I provide another challenge. Other times a student's response is correct, but he or she seems unsure. And at times I present another challenge so that a student who is thinking erroneously can find a different way to reach the solution.

Becky was typical of those students who reasoned that the colors would be the same. She wrote: *I think they would be the same color because in A you have 1 yellow and 2 red. In B you have 2 yellow and 3 red. There is always 1 more red than yellow, so B should have more contents but A and B are the same color.*

I wrote several more problems on Becky's paper. One of them was to compare the following:

Becky explained why she thought that these two mixtures would be the same color. She wrote: *I think that A and B are the same color because in A there is half as much yellow than there is red, and in B, there is half as much yellow than there is red too. A has more contents but they're the same color.*

I then asked Becky to rethink the original problem. She stuck with her first analysis that they were the same color. Becky's paper reminded me that partial understanding is part of the learning process. She needed additional experiences and more time to think about problems like these. (See Becky's work on the following page.)

Some of the students' solutions revealed that they were able to reason proportionally. David, for example, wrote: *A would be darker than B because there is twice as much red than yellow. In B there should be four red to make them the same color.*

Leeann's reasoning was similar to David's. She wrote: *I think colunm A is darker because in colunm A there are twice as many reds than yellows so in colunm B for it to be the same it would have to have four Reds instead.*

Becky argued incorrectly that the colors were the same because each was one more part red than yellow. Although she was able to reason correctly for two other examples, she maintained her position for the first problem. (Grade 5)

I think they would be the same color because in A you have 1 yellow and 2 red. In B you have 2 yellow and 3 red. There is always 1 more red than yellow, so B should have more contents but A and B are the same color

Becky - Suppose you had 100 cans of red paint and only one can of yellow. If you mixed these together, how would the color compare with the mixtures in # 1 and 2 above? Please explain.

#3 would be alot darker than #1 and 2 because in 1 and 2 there are almost the same amount of yellow cans than red cans but in #3 there is not nearly as much yellow than red so since #3 has 99% red and 1% yellow, #3 is definately darker.

Becky - what about these?

I think that A and B are the same color because in A, there is half as much yellow than there is red, and in B, there is half as much yellow than there is red too. A has more contents but they're the same color.

Becky - I agree. Now - what about these? Compare with what you just wrote. Are they the same?

yes, I do think they are the same color because there is always 1 more red than yellow.

"Am I right?" Leeann asked me after I read her paper.

"Your reasoning makes good sense to me," I responded. Because I was curious about her uncertainty, I wrote another problem for her to solve:

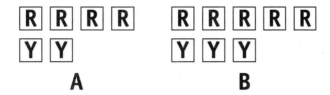

Leeann's analysis confirmed her understanding. She wrote: *I think colunm A is darker because in colunm A there are twice as many reds than yellows, so in colunm B for it to be the same it would have to have 6 reds instead of 5.*

> ᴬ R R Y ᴮ R R R Y Y
>
> I think colunm A is darker because in colunm A there are twice as many reds than yellows so in colunm B for it to be the same it would have to have four Reds instead.
> _____
> Leeann — What about these?
> R R R R   R R R R R
> Y Y   Y Y Y
> _____
> I think colunm A is darker because in colunm A there are twice as many reds than yellows, so in colunm B for it to be the same it would have to have 6 reds instead of 5.

Leeann correctly analyzed the colors in the two samples, and then correctly analyzed another problem. (Grade 5)

Daria referred to fractions in her solution to the initial problem. She wrote: *I think A would be darker because A has double the amount of red than yellow and B has only ¾ more red than yellow. Yellow is lighter than red. Neither one would be balanced perfectly.* Because her reasoning about ¾ wasn't clear to me, I gave Daria two other mixtures to compare. I was curious to see if she would refer to fractions again. I wrote on her paper:

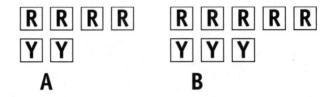

Daria's response showed her confusion. She wrote: *I think A would be the same as B but this confuses me because of what I wrote for number 1 . . I can go either way!*

After I read this, I asked her to write some more to help me understand her thinking. She added: *Attually I think A would be darker for the same reason as 1. A again has double the amount of reds than B and B has less reds than yellow.*

I think A would be darker because. A has double the amount of red than yellow and B has only 3/4 more red than yellow. Yellow is lighter than red. Neither one would be balanced perfectly.

Daria — What about this one? Please explain.

I think A would be the same as B but, this confuses me because of what I wrote for number 1 .. I can go either way!

Attually I think A would be darker for the same reason as 1. A again has double the amount of reds than B and B has less reds. than yellow.

Daria wrote about her confusion in thinking about the problems. (Grade 5)

I find that written dialogues with students not only give me insights into their thinking and reasoning processes but also help me revisit their thinking later. Their papers are extremely helpful for assessing their understanding and making plans for follow-up lessons.

The next day, I asked for volunteers to read their papers aloud, and the argument continued. To follow up, I asked the students to create other similar paint mixture problems and solve them. Then the students exchanged papers and solved one another's problems. Their discussions were animated, and more of the students began to understand the power of reasoning proportionally.

Courtney created a problem and analyzed it correctly. (Grade 5)

I think A would be darker because there has to be twice as much red as yellow so in B there would have to be six Red to make it the same color as A.

Jennifer used erroneous reasoning for the problem she created. (Grade 5)

I think that they would be the same because there is 2 more red than yellow in A + B except there is more paint in B.

Wesley compared three cans of paint in the problem he created. (Grade 5)

I think A is darkest because there is twice as much red as yellow in C there is just a little bit more red then yellow. B there is not twice as much red as yellow.

Division (Grade 3)

Near the end of a unit on division, I was interested in finding out how the third graders would deal with solving a division problem in various contexts, and I was particularly interested in how the children would express the remainders. I asked the children to figure the answer to 21 divided by 4 and presented them with four different situations:

1. Divide 21 balloons among 4 people.
2. Divide 21 cookies among 4 people.
3. Divide $21.00 among 4 people.
4. Divide 21 by 4 on a calculator.

I asked the students to record their answers and explain why the answer for each problem made sense. I didn't have them discuss the problem before they wrote. Nor did I use the students' solutions for a later class discussion. Instead, I used the assignment as an assessment to see how individual children would respond.

All but three of the students were able to solve the problems. However, they explained their answers in different ways. Brandon, for example, solved the problem of the extra balloon by giving it away.

Brandon solved each problem correctly and explained his reasoning. (Grade 3)

Tanya brought her paper to me after she solved each problem. For the first three, she drew pictures to help her figure the answers. For the fourth problem, she wrote the numbers as if they were on a calculator display. I reminded Tanya that she had to explain why each answer made sense. She added: *1. This answer made sence to me because you can split a cookie up. 2. This answer made sence to me because you can't split up a balloon. 3. This answer made sence to me because first I gave them eaqual amounts in dollars. There was one dollar left, so I split it into four, and that is 25¢. 4. I did it on the calculator.*

Tanya solved the problems, but at first didn't give explanations; she added them afterward. (Grade 3)

Andrew was the only student in the class who explained his first answer by adding 5¼ four times. (Grade 3)

21 ÷ 4

1) Sharing cookies,
each person will get 5 cookies
and ¼ of a cookie becuase 5¼ + 5¼
5¼ + 5¼ = 21

2) Sharing balloons. each person
gets 5 balloons and there will
be 1 left becuas 5 + 5 + 5 + 5 + 1
= 21

3) sharing $21.00 each
person gets $5.25 becuase
$5.25 + $5.25 + $5.25 + $5.25
= 21 dollars

5.25

4) Useing calculater it says
5.25 becuase the calculater
showed me.

Josh added his own brand of humor to his paper. (Grade 3)

21 ÷ 4

1) Each person gets 5¼ cookies
becuase you can cut cookies
becuasee the sweet called cookies
can be cut up

2) Each child gets 5 ballons
and one of the balloons gose
to there dog Rut
the onser makes sence because
dogs like ballons too

3) Each person gets $5.25 because
1 dollar can be split into 1, 2, 4, 5, 10, 20
and a lot more

4) I would do 21 ÷ 4 =
and I will get 5.25 I think
Yes I did get 5.25 that means
that the answer is 5 and a quarter
I know that is true because
calculacelers almose never are wrong
auchlly never wrong

The Pizza Problem (Grades 7 and 8)

Some teachers like to give problems as homework assignments, presenting them early in the week and giving the students until Friday to solve them. These "Problems of the Week" give students assignments that challenge them to face problem situations that are new to them and engage them in thinking and reasoning. At times, a POW, as a Problem of the Week is sometimes called, relates to the mathematics students are working on in class; at other times, it deals with an area of math that the students have either already studied or will be studying shortly.

When teaching a unit on the area of circles, I asked a class of seventh and eighth grade students to investigate the prices of different sizes of pizzas to see if the prices were related to the pizzas' areas. "What you're to do," I said, "is to phone a pizza place and find out how big each size pizza is and how much it costs. Then figure whether the prices relate to their sizes. If they do, explain why. If not, explain what the prices would be if they were proportional to their areas."

The students were used to getting Problems of the Week in written form, but I didn't prepare these directions in writing. Instead, I asked that each student write the problem in his or her own words. In this way, I took the opportunity to give the students experience with formulating a problem in writing. I gave them time to do this and then had several students read what they had written.

Amanda wrote: *Call up a pizza place & ask the size of each of their pizzas in inches, small medium, or large. Then ask the prices. See if the prices are proportional to the areas of the pizzas. If they are not, reprice them.*

Allison wrote: *Call or visit a pizza place. Find out the size and price of pizzas. Then decide whether it's mathematically sensible or not. How much would you charge?*

Geoff wrote: *What are the prices of a small, medium, and large pizza? Do they make mathematical sense? If so, why? If not, what should they charge?*

Jennifer wrote: *What we are supposed to do is to call or visit a pizza place, and find out what the price of each pizza is and what size it is. We then have to decide whether or not the prices are acceptable. If they aren't, what would we change them to?*

Most of the students figured the area of each pizza in square inches and then figured out how much a square inch of pizza cost for each size. In most cases, the larger pizzas were less expensive per square inch. Some students decided the prices were close enough and were fine. Others presented alternative pricing.

> What are the prices of a small, medium and large pizza? Do they make mathematical sense? If so why? If not ~~what~~ what ld should they charge?

> *P.O.W.*
>
> Call up a pizza place & ask the size of each of their pizzas in inches small, medium, or large. Then ask the prices. See if the prices are proportional to the areas of the pizzas. If they are not, reprice them.

Students formulated the pizza problem in different ways. (Grade 7)

Jacob, for example, concluded: *The deference in price is minimal when you look at it on a small scale but if you were going to buy fifty thousand square inches of pizza for a big party you were having while you're parents were away for the weekend then you would have to consider what size pizza would be the most economical.*

Mike had a different approach to economizing. He wrote: *Skimp on the toppings.*

The students' solutions and explanations revealed their understanding not only about the area of circles but also about other mathematical ideas. They were interested in the different prices and sizes from different pizza places, and the problem was a good way to relate the mathematics they were learning to the world outside of school.

POW/PIZZA

The first thing I did was to call
Primos Pizza. I found that their
small pizza costs $5.40 and
it is 10 inches in diameter. I also
found the medium is $7.30 and 12
inches in diameter. Last but not
least the large cheese pizza which
costs $8.75 and is 14 inches in
diameter.

By dividing the diameter by 2 I
got the radius. I multiplied this by π
I got the total area or total amount
of sq. in's.
For small I got 78.5 sq. in

$$\frac{\$}{sq. in.} \quad \frac{540}{78.5}$$

For medium I got 113 sq. in.

$$\frac{\$}{sq. in.} \quad \frac{730}{113}$$

For large I got 153.86 sq. in.

$$\frac{\$}{sq. in.} \quad \frac{875}{153.86}$$

Next I divided each cost by
the area or sq. in's.

small - $78.5\overline{)540}$ = 6.878 or 6.9¢ sq in.

medium - $113\overline{)730}$ = 6.46 or 6.5¢ sq. in.

large - $153.86\overline{)875}$ = 5.656 or 5.7 ¢
$= 7$ sq. in.

---

the cost per square inch really
suprised me. Because, really
all of the prices per sq. in.
went down. Really, the bigger a
pizza gets the higher the
price. along with the size.
These pizzas went up 2 inches in
diameter along with about 2 inches
in price each one. when the
final sq. in. price went down
from small to large I thought it strange.
If I owned a pizza place
I would make sure that there
was a slight bargain for buying
a large yet not a total decrease
in price.

In her solution, Amanda discovered that the three different sizes of pizzas weren't priced in proportion to their areas, but she didn't recommend prices. (Grade 8)

P.O.W.

THE POW FOR THIS WEEK INSTRUCTED US TO CALL A PIZZA PLACE
AND FIND OUT THE DIAMETER AND PRICE OF EACH OF THEIR PIZZAS.
FROM THEIR WE WERE SUPPOSED TO FIND OUT IF THE PRICES WERE
PROPORTIONAL TO THE SIZES. , IF THEY WERE NOT WE WERE TO MAKE UP
OUR OWN PRICES FOR THE DIAMETER SO THEY WOULD BE PROPORTIONAL.
I CALLED A DOMINOES IN SAN RAFEL AND GOT THE FOLLOWING
INFORMATION -

	price	diameter
	$7.00	12 inches
	$9.75	16 inches

MY NEXT STEP WAS TO FIND OUT HOW MUCH EACH SO INCH OF PIZZA
COST.

PRICE	DIVIDED BY	PI R2
$7.00	divided by	3.14 X 36
$7.00	divided by	113.04

makes about 6¢ a sq inch of pizza
NOW I NEEDED TO SEE IF THE LARGER PIZZA ALSO COST 6¢ A SQ
INCH OF PIZZA SO I DID THE SAME STEPS FOR THIS LARGER PIZZA.

PRICE	DIVIDED BY	PI R2
$9.75	divided by	3.14 X 64
$9.75	divided by	200.96

makes about 5¢ a sq inch of pizza
AS YOU CAN SEE THIS PIZZA PLACE IS GIVING YOU A DEAL WHEN YOU GET
A LARGER SIZED PIZZA.
BUT FOR THE SAKE OF ARGUEMENT I'M SUPPOSED TO FIND A PRICE SO
THAT THE PIZZAS WILL BE PROPORTIONAL TO THE SIZES.
the way to do this is to set up theproblem needed to be solved

PRICE	DIVIDED BY	PI R2
?	DIVIDED BY	3.14 X 64
?	divided by	200.96

i noticed that 200.96 is a little less than doubling
114.04 (the area of the smaller pizza) so i figured th price
should be a little less than doubling the smaller pizza's price
I TRIED $13.00 AND DIVIDED IT BY @)).(¢ TO GET ABOUT 6¢ PER SQ
INCH OF PIZZA.

IF THIS PIZZA PLACE WAS MINE THE 12 INCH PIZZA WOULD COST $7.00
WHILE THE 16 INCH PIZZA COST $13.00.

After analyzing the prices, Jennifer suggested a new price for a 12-inch pizza. (Grade 7)

Explaining Mathematical Ideas

Some of the most mathematically interesting pieces of writing I've received from students have been when I've asked them to write about specific mathematical concepts. In assignments like these, students present a view into their thinking about mathematics that gives me information that I find intriguing, sometimes surprising, and usually helpful for assessing their understanding.

I've found several ways to structure these assignments. Sometimes I make a straightforward request and ask the students to write what they know about an idea. I might ask, "Write about what division is" or "Write all you know about angles." I often have a brief discussion first so that the students can express their ideas orally. Talking about their ideas makes it easier for students to begin to put their thoughts in writing.

I consistently remind students that I am the audience for their writing, that their papers tell me if they understood what I was teaching. As with all assignments, I encourage them to include as much detail as possible.

What Is Subtraction? (Grade 3)

I've found that children have difficulty learning that subtraction relates to different kinds of situations. When I teach subtraction, I give students experiences with three different subtraction situations—taking away one quantity from another (for example, Tanya has eight pennies and gives two to her sister, Leticia), comparing the difference between two quantities (for example, Paul has nine pennies and Sam has four), and figuring out how many more are needed (for example, Billy has nine pennies and wants to buy an eraser that costs 19 cents). It typically takes many experiences for children to learn to identify all of these and to represent them numerically as subtraction situations.

When I asked third graders to write a paper titled "What Is Subtraction?" Brian's paper showed his understanding of the three types of subtraction situations. He wrote: *Subtraction is numbers. You need it wen you have 8 apples and and you eat two I use suptrachen to see how many apples are left. You can almost use sudtrachen any time or place. I used it when I trade my base ball cards and my vido game to see how many more ponts I get. I got fifty pounts and the next time I played it I got one hunded and I use suptrachen for the aswer and the aswer is I got fifty more pounts on my second game than my first Game. You have an hour to do some thing and you did it in twelv minet & you use suptrathion to see how much time you have left.*

1 what is
Subtraction?

Subtraction is numbers.
You need it wen you
have 8 apples and and
you eat two I use suptrachen
to sea how many
apples are left.
You can almost
use sudtrachen
iny timor place. I used
it when I trade
my base ball cards and
my vido game to see
how many more ponts I get.
I got fifty pounts

2

and the next time
I played it I got
one hunded and I use
suptrachen for the
aswer and the aswer
is I got fifty more
pountson my second
game than my
first Game. You have
an hour to do
some thing and you
did it intwelv minete
you use suptrathiou to see
how much time you
have left.

Brian explained how subtraction relates to several different kinds of problems. (Grade 3)

Most children, however, wrote only about subtraction as taking away. Janie, for example, wrote: *I think subtraction is takeing away something from something. If you are going shoping and you boght some things and the price was ten* <u>*dollars*</u> *but you only have a twenty dollar bill. So you give the person at the counter the twenty dollar bill and he subracts ten dollars from twenty dollars (because ten plus ten is twenty) and gives you ten dollars back.*

What Is Subtraction

I think subtraction is takeing away something from something. If you are going shoping and you boght some things and the price was ten <u>dollars</u> but you only have a twenty dollar bill. So you give the person at the counter the twenty dollar bill and he subtracts ten dollars from twenty dollars (because ten plus ten is twenty) and gives you ten dollars back. Or if you went <u>somewere</u> to buy twenty six pumpkins for your class because there were twenty six kids in your class but by mistake you boght 30 sp you had to subtract four pumpkins from the 30 pumpkins to make twenty six.

Janie described subtraction as "taking away something from something" and also showed how addition relates to subtraction. (Grade 3)

James struggled with writing, but his paper showed that he grasped the concept of subtraction. He wrote: *Subtraction is opers* [opposite] *of adding. Subtraction is like daved* [dividing]. *ervey day people use subtraction. I will do subtraction rithe* [right] *now.* James showed how he would subtract 41 from 93. (His work appears on the next page.)

When I read the students' papers, I realized that I needed to provide them with additional opportunities to see that problems of "comparing" and "how many more" can be represented and solved by subtraction.

Writing was difficult for James,
but he worked to explain what
he knew about subtraction.
(Grade 3)

What is Subtraction?
Subtraction is <u>opers</u> [opposite] of
adding. subtraction is like
<u>daved</u> [dividing]. ervey day people
use subtraction. I will
do subtraction <u>rithe</u> [right]
now.

$$\begin{array}{r} 93 \\ -41 \\ \hline 52 \end{array}$$

subtraction is not
a <u>lillt</u> [little] sén [sign]
Like this oew.

X   +

Tanya expressed her unique
view of subtraction.
(Grade 3)

Tuesday Pizza Day
and Juice Bar Day
Yummy!   What is Subtracktion?
I think subtraction is a <u>mathmatical</u> art of
<u>creativety</u> Taking away is the main idea of
subtraction creativety. I use subtraction when
I eat. You are subtracting when you eat
each bite. <u>Mathmatics</u> and <u>creativety</u> aren't
always in subtraction. Subtraction thinking
sometimes, like when you're doing work-book-
math. For a sample: 13-11=2 or 16-3=13,
Things like that. When it's creative/mathmatical
art, that's diffrent. If you really think
about it, you are subtracting words from
your head (sortes) and <u>erasing</u> [or] is subtraction.

Chance and Strategy (Grade 2)

In a probability unit with second graders, I taught the children a collection of games and talked with them about the difference between games of chance and games that involved strategy. I wanted to relate the ideas of chance and strategy to experiences from the children's lives outside of school as well as to their classroom learning.

I began class one day by posting chart paper and ruling it into three columns titled "Strategy," "Chance," and "Both Strategy and Chance."

"Think about games that you play both here in class and at home that I can write on this chart," I said. "When you pick one to report, decide in which column it belongs."

Practically every child's hand shot up to volunteer a game. However, many were unsure about in which column each game belonged, and the children engaged in a great deal of back-and-forth dialogue. The discussions were animated. After about 35 minutes, I had listed the following games on the chart:

Strategy	Chance	Both
Chess	Chutes & Ladders	Sorry
Checkers	Row Sham Bow	Aggravation
Go to the Head	Roll 2 Dice	Crazy 8s
of the Class		The 1 to 10 Game
Password		Monopoly
Timber		Slam Basket
Four-in-a-Row		Clue
Operation		Poker
		Blackjack
		Pop Go Perfection
		Roll 15
		Nintendo

The next day, I gave the class a writing assignment. I told the children that they were to explain what chance and strategy were and give examples of games in each category on the chart. I wrote on the board:

Chance, Strategy, or Both

1. Chance means _____.
2. Strategy means _____.
3. A game that is just chance is _____ because

_____.

4. A game that is both chance and strategy is _____ because

_____.

I told the children that they didn't have to number their sentences or write them in this order. "Also," I said, "you can change the words if you want, as long as your paper explains what you know about chance and strategy."

Some of the students got right to work, but there were questions and confusion from about half of the children. When I helped these children, I had them tell me their ideas, and then I told them to write down those words on paper. The more writing experiences children have, the more they realize that the words they write on paper come from the words they think about or say aloud.

The assignment took most of the children the entire class period to complete, and their papers were varied. Teddy wrote: *chance is maybe. strategy is there is a way you can like figure it out. Both is like it is half strategy and half chance. shake and peek is a chance game because you cannot control where the marbel gowes. I do not think eny one game is strategy. Likley unlikley is both becaus you can do a cheet roll.* Teddy had argued throughout the unit that he could control the dice to get certain rolls.

Catherine wrote: *Chance mens it can hapin or it cudent. Strategy mens you hafto think in your head. Roll 2 Dise is a chance game becaues the dice controls the dice. Roll 15 is strategy in it because yore bran [brain] tells you wat you shuold do.*

From Nick: *Chance means when your not shor [sure]. Strategy means when you have a plan. A game that is just chance [is] peek boxes because*

Nick understood that strategy involves having some control over a game. (Grade 2)

> Chance, Strategy, or both
>
> Chance means when your not shor.
> Strategy means when you have a plan
> A game that is just chance
> peek boxes because you can't cantroll
> the mare boll that gos in the corner.
> A game that has strateay and
> chance the 1 to 10 game
> because you antcan troll the dice
> bot you can can troll the cards.

you cant cantroll the mareboll that go's in the corner. A game that has strategay and chance [is] the 1 to 10 game because you can't cantroll the dice bot you can cantroll the cards.

From Katy: *Chance means you don't have a clue what your going to get. Strategy means you have a plan for somethig. I think Empty the bowl # 1, 2, 3 are just chance. I think Roll 15 is chance and strategy because you don'n know what your going to get but you can choose witch die your goig [going] to use.*

Chance, Strategey or Both,
Chance means you don't have a clue what your going to get. Strategy means you have a plan for some thig.
I think Empty the bowl # 1,2,3 are just chance.
I think Roll 15 is chance and strategy because you don'n know what your going to get but you can choose witch die your goig to use.

Katy seemed to understand the difference between chance and strategy. (Grade 2)

Grace wrote: *Chance means there is no thinking. The dice control it. Strategy means you need to think. A game that is just chance is Roll two dice because dice is the only thing to control the game. You never know whitch numbers going to win. A game that has strategy and chance is roll 15 because you get to choose the dice and you never know what numbers are going to come out and you can stop when you want to.*

From Rudy: *Chance is when you don't know what is going happin. Strategy is when you know what is going to happin. A game with both is the 1 to 10 game because you roll the dice and you can't control the dice and you pick witch cards to put down. A game with just chance is it ten? because you just turn over the cards.*

From Leslie: *Chance is when you are not sure what will happen. Strategy is when you have to think alot. A game that is just chance is Roll 2 Dice. A game that is strategy is Roll 15 because it has alot of both. The chance part is the dice. And the strategy part is the adding. You can stay with what you have or you can keep on rolling. You can't control the DICE!!*

Chance, Strategy or Both

Chance is when you are not sure what will happen.
Strategy is when you have to think alot.
A game that is just chance is Roll 2 Dice.
A game that is just strategy is Roll 15 because it has a lot of both. The chance...

part is the dice.
And the strategy part is the adding. You can stay with what you have or you can keep on rolling.
You can't control the DICE!!

Leslie knew that strategy called for thinking. (Grade 2)

Compared to their other writing assignments, these second graders had written a great deal. I think there were two reasons for this: They had had the chance to talk about their ideas before writing, and they were able to relate the topic to experiences outside of school as well as to what they were learning in class.

Using Protractors (Grades 7 and 8)

From her past experiences teaching middle school students about angles, Cathy Humphreys knew that students often have difficulty learning how to use protractors. Often they don't see the need for the tool, so Cathy does not introduce protractors until after the students have had concrete experiences measuring angles several ways.

When Cathy distributed protractors to her class in San Jose, California, she told the students, "The protractor is a useful tool for both measuring angles and drawing angles of specific sizes." She asked the students to work in pairs and explore the protractors.

"It may be helpful to use a right angle as a reference," she suggested, "since you already know a right angle is 90 degrees."

After a while, Cathy called the class to attention and asked the students to share what they had noticed. Then Cathy gave them the challenge of figuring out how to use the protractors and writing directions that someone else could follow. She said, "Your directions should tell how to measure angles and also how to draw angles of different sizes. You can include drawings if they will help make your directions clear."

Before the students began, Cathy wrote *protractor* and *angle* on the overhead for their reference and asked them what other words about angles they might use. She listed all the words the students suggested: *acute, right, obtuse, straight, degrees.*

Students expressed their thinking in different ways. Jenny and Sara, for example, wrote the following directions for measuring an angle: *First, you make an angle. Then you place the bottom line of the angle on the line of the protractor. Then you put the dot on the vertex of the angle. Then you find out what degree the angle is. If you can't figure it out, you do this. First you find out if your angle is obtuse or acute. If it's obtuse you use the top line, if it's acute you use the bottom line. Then you get the arrow and take it up to the number and the number that the line hits is the degree of your angle.*

Cuong and Cheryl wrote: *One rule you must always remember is you must always have the bulls eye on the straight line on the bottom. If the angle goes to the right you must read the bottom numbers. But if it goes to the left you must read the top numbers.*

Ron M. and Ron S. wrote: *You place the vertex of the angle you are measuring in the middle of the hole. The hole is on the bottom of the protractor. When measuring, let's say that it is 69 degrees. On the protractor it does not say 69°. Only 50, 60, & 70. What you do is measure and count by the lines on top of the protractor.*

Will and Pat designed their work as a pamphlet. They titled it *The Protractor Manual*. They wrote: *There are 2 things a Protrator does for you. it 1. measures angles and 2. It makes new angles. To measure an angle you put the rough side of the protractor down then put the vertex of the angle in the little hole in the middle, (shown on page 2) and if the angle is acute you use the numbers on the bottom on the right but if it is acute but it is pointing to the left you use the left side and the top. (shown on page 2) To make angles you use the bottom part of the Protractor (shown on Page 2) to make any angle you disire.*

Students explained in different ways how to use a protractor. (Grades 7-8)

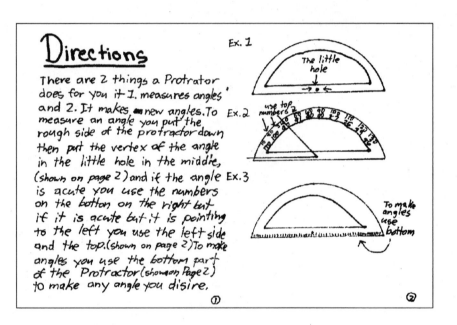

Directions

There are 2 things a Protrator does for you it 1. measures angles and 2. It makes new angles. To measure an angle you put the rough side of the protractor down then put the vertex of the angle in the little hole in the middle, (shown on page 2) and if the angle is acute you use the numbers on the bottom on the right but if it is acute but it is pointing to the left you use the left side and the top. (shown on page 2) To make angles you use the bottom part of the Protractor (shown on Page 2) to make any angle you disire.

Ex. 1   The little hole

Ex. 2   use top numbers

Ex. 3   To make angles use bottom

step 1 - measuring

place the protractor on your paper where the angle is where you see the vertex put it in the center circle. to find the degrees use the numbers closest to the half circle and there you have it, an measured angle.

step 2 - drawing

after you place the protractor on the paper, place a dot in the center circle. from the dot draw a straight line to . then look at the degrees closest to the half circle. draw a straight line from the vertex to the degrees. then (hopefully) you drew an angle.

Comparing Fractions (Grade 5)

After working with fractions for several weeks in a class of fifth graders, I asked the students to explain which was larger—$\frac{2}{3}$ or $\frac{3}{4}$. In addition to answering the question, the students were to indicate whether the question was too easy, just right, or too hard. The papers gave me insights into how the students thought about fractions and also provided the basis for a class discussion about the students' different views.

Some students drew pictures to help explain their reasoning. Sarah, for example, drew two 3-by-4 rectangles and shaded in eight squares on one and nine on the other. She wrote: *$\frac{3}{4}$ cover 9 pieces out of twelve and $\frac{2}{3}$ cover 8 pieces out of twelve.*

Sarah thought the problem of explaining why 3/4 was larger than 2/3 was too easy. (Grade 5)

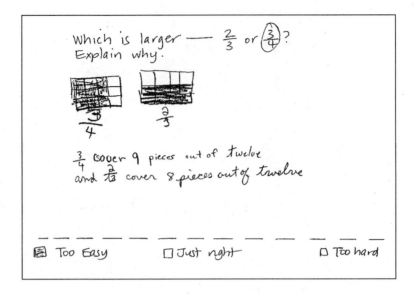

Which is larger — $\frac{2}{3}$ or $\frac{3}{4}$? Explain why.

$\frac{3}{4}$ cover 9 pieces out of twelve
and $\frac{2}{3}$ cover 8 pieces out of twelve

☒ Too Easy   ☐ Just right   ☐ Too hard

Alex also decided to draw, but he drew two circles, dividing each into 12 segments. Alex was an extremely capable math student, and he knew that ¾ was larger. However, his drawing didn't help him explain why, and he was frustrated. He checked the box "Too hard" and added: *to explain.*

Alex was frustrated by trying to explain the problem. (Grade 5)

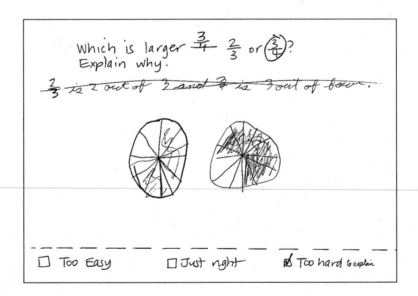

Which is larger $\frac{3}{4}$ $\frac{2}{3}$ or $\frac{3}{4}$? Explain why.

$\frac{2}{3}$ is 2 out of 3 and $\frac{3}{4}$ is 3 out of four.

☐ Too Easy   ☐ Just right   ☒ Too hard to explain

Many children find it easier to deal with fractions that have numerators of 1. Alison found a way to use ⅓ and ¼ to explain her reasoning. She wrote: *⅔ out of a circle leave ⅓. ¾ out of a circle leave ¼. ⅓ is bigger than ¼. If ⅓ takes up more room than ¼ than ¾ is oviously bigger.* Alison felt the problem was just right.

Damien's paper was unique. He wrote: *The pizza is divide into 4s. ⅓ is 1⅓ of ¼. When it is ⅔ it will be 2⅔ of ¼. The 2 = 2¼ and ⅔ is ⅔ of ¼. But it said ¾ and 2¼ = 2/4 and ¾ of the ¼ still doesn't equals to ¾.* I had to make sketches in order to figure out how Damien had reasoned!

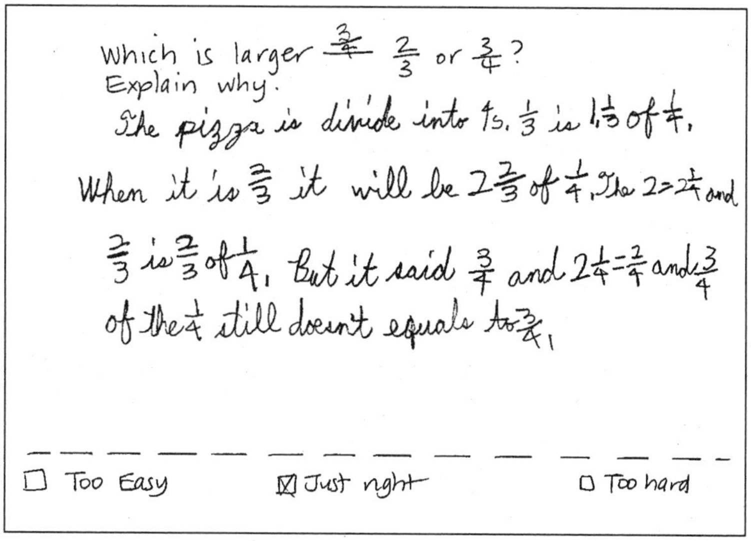

Which is larger $\frac{3}{4}$ $\frac{2}{3}$ or $\frac{3}{4}$? Explain why.

The pizza is divide into 4s. ⅓ is 1⅓ of ¼. When it is ⅔ it will be 2⅔ of ¼. The 2 = 2¼ and ⅔ is ⅔ of ¼. But it said ¾ and 2¼ = 2/4 and ¾ of the ¼ still doesn't equals to ¾.

☐ Too Easy   ☑ Just right   ☐ Too hard

Damien's reasoning was complex, but correct. (Grade 5)

Writing Before and After—Circles (Grade 6)

Sometimes I have students write about their ideas at the beginning of a unit and then again at the end. In this way, both the students and I have the chance to see what they've learned.

For example, I taught a two-week unit in which sixth-graders experimented with six different methods for approximating the area of a circle. At the beginning of the unit, I asked the students to write what they knew about circles. Most of the students' papers indicated that they knew the parts of the circle. Michelle's paper was typical. She drew a circle with a diameter and a radius and wrote: *A circle has no faces. The line going straight through the center is called the diameter. The line going from the top to the center is called a radius. The outside of the circle is called the circumference.*

Chris included a few other facts as well. He wrote: *Circles have 360°. The diameter of a circle is the distance across it going across the middle. The radius of a circle is the distance From the middle of it to the end. The circumference is the distance around a circle. If you take any circle and divide its circumference by its diameter you will get pie.*

Some students included other information. Jeff, for example, wrote: *A circle is an object that has no sides and is 360 degrees around. It is round* and if you put a point in the middle and measure to the outside it is the same distance all around. Circles are in many diferent things such as coke cans or some bottles. Circles are used in pie graphs. Without the invention of the circle we would still be in the stone age.

Katy wrote: *A circle is an object that has a round apprence [appearance]. All points are the same distantice as the center point. It is a very useful item we use it every day for cars, trucks, biycicles, gears. It is also the dimension of planets and stars.*

At the end of the unit, I asked the students to write what they had learned about circles. Their papers helped me assess what the unit had accomplished and understand how different students had responded to it. Despite our best teaching efforts, the taught curriculum and the experienced curriculum are not always the same.

Michael wrote: *This was a good asignment because it expanded our minds to find different ways to find the area of a circle instead of doing the old mathematical way. The ways we did the methods were wierd. I never thought we could do it. but doing this project is good communication. We did it with partners so we learned to work together and learn the new methods.*

I learned about that if you shuffle pieces around you could make an easier object to find the area. Like in the curvy parallelagram method we shuffled the pieces around to make an easier object.

Cory wrote: *I really never knew their was so many ways to find out the area of a circle. I learned about circumscribing, inscribing, weighing a circle made out of linoleum, how to find the area with beans, centimeters squared, and how it has to do with a circle, averaging numbers, counting squares and then averaging those numbers together, and experimenting with all these things.*

I'm sure that everybody has written this. "I have learned what the area of a circle is which is $\pi \times r^2$." But a teacher just didn't say it when he/she was in the front of the class. They proved it and thats one of the things that makes this project so special.

Jason wrote: *What I learned from this project was how to work better with people and get along with them better. I also learned how to find the area of a circle in a couple of fun and exciting ways. Such as weighing, counting, etc. I really don't know when I'll have to use this skill, but I guess its a good skill to have.*

From Lauren: *I learned a lot of ways to find the area of a circle. I was especially amazed that you could find the area of a circle by weighing. I mean that nobody would think of finding an area by weighing, they would rather think of multipling or something more mathematical.*

I learned that you can take something apart and put it back together in a different shape and that could help you find the area of something (like the curvy parellogram method). The same area can be found if you take something apart and put it back together in a different shape.

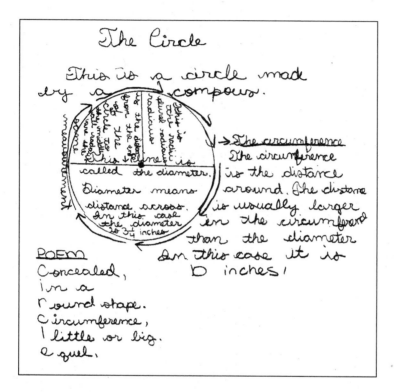

In her beginning paper, Lauren labeled the radius, diameter, and circumference. She measured them and wrote a poem. At the end of the unit, she focused on two of the methods she had used for finding the area of a circle. (Grade 6)

In his first paper, Chris focused on the facts he knew about circles. He wrote his end-of-the-unit paper from a different perspective. (Grade 6)

What I know about

CIRCLES have 360°.
The diameter of a circle is the distance across it going across the middle.
The radius of a circle is the distance from the middle of it to the end.
The circumference is the distance around a circle.
If you take any circle and divide its circumference by its diameter you will get pie.

Circles

Math
Circle

What I learned from this

Me and Jeff were partners on an experiment to find the area of circle. We were given six methods to experiment with.
After we completed the experiment I thought that the experiment really did teach me a lot.
One thing was that there is <u>always</u> more than one method in finding the answer in mathmatics.
That was proven by the six different methods to find the circles area.
I also learned that finding the area of a circle isn't impossible (even though that is what I thought before).
I learned the methods themselves for finding the area of a circle.

More Writing Before and After—Geometry (Grade 3)

When Cheryl Rectanus taught a geometry unit to third graders in Piedmont, California, she began the unit by asking the students to write what they knew about geometry. She explained that they would read these papers again at the end of the unit and write about what they had learned.

The children's writing revealed a range of understanding about geometry. Julie, for example, wrote: *I dont no about gomrty xsept shaps. I like nubers bettr.*

Tanya seemed to have a more complete view of geometry. She wrote: *Geometry is shapes and angles and sizes. You have geometry in your house. Your bed is a shape (rectangl) and cookies are round. And my sister said you have angles on shapes.*

George wrote: *it can be fun and it can be borring but I like it. it pretty much it can be like art in numeres ways. it . . . it really you no how many shapes are in the world infinity!!!! thats all I no.*

Elena, who was often vocal about her dislike of numbers, wrote: *I prefer shap's better then number's because numbers are sort of difficult for me. I like shap's because you can do so meny thing's with them.*

At the end of the unit, Cheryl said to the class, "When we began this unit, we talked together about geometry and then you wrote about what you knew about geometry. You've all learned a lot since we began, and I'm interested in reading what you know about geometry now. It will help me understand more about you and will also give me information so I'll know if the activities you did could be helpful for teaching other children about geometry." She reviewed briefly the unit's class lessons and individual activities.

"I'd like you to read the first papers you wrote about geometry and then write what you know now," Cheryl explained. "When you write, include how you felt about the unit and what you know now. Add any other information you think will help me understand you and your thinking."

Kendra wrote: *I learned lots of new geometry words like: 3 dimensional, prism, rectangular prism, faces, vertices/vertix, eges and (my favorite) parrallelepiped. I think 3rd graders should study geometry because you can't teach an old dog new tricks. Geometry is important because theres shapes all around us and if we didn't know what to call them or how to identify them, we would not have strutures, meaning houses, briges, buildings, mostly anything.*

Emma also had a global view of geometry: *I learned that geometry isn't just a bunch of shapes, I understand now that geometry is in everything from the wall of the room to a leftover candy wrapper. I also know that if you aren't persistent with finding shapes you aren't going to find what you want to. I also learned that geometry can be fun for all ages.*

When you introduced this subject I thought it was going to be imensly boring and not worth while, But now I have a second thought—I noticed that nothing in this class has been boring especially geometry!

I also know some thing I didn't know before, that you can turn one shape into another.

As well as learning about geometry, Grant felt he had learned an important social skill. (Grade 3)

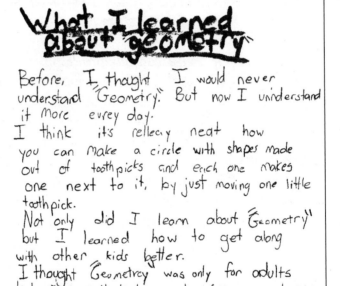

What I learned about geometry

Before, I thought I would never understand "Geometry". But now I understand it more evrey day.
I think it's relleay neat how you can make a circle with shapes made out of toothpicks and each one makes one next to it, by just moving one little toothpick.
Not only did I learn about "Geometry" but I learned how to get along with other kids better.
I thought Geometray was only for odults but now I think it can be for anyne at any time and any age starting at 6.

Many students commented about specific concepts they had learned. Tom wrote: *I learned what convex was. I learned what polygons are. I learned what octagon was and decagon and nongan and concave and a lot more shapes and how they form.*

Justin wrote: *1. I learned that some words mean the same as others, for example, faces and sides. 2. I learned that it's not always best to be alone. A partner sometimes thinks a different way and gets other answers. 3. I learned that learning and experimenting with shapes can be fun. 4. I learned that sometimes you have to think ahead. For instance, in the Put-in-Order Problem you have to say to yourself, "if I put this shape down, can it turn in to this shape?" 5. I learned that you have to look closely at some shapes because they might be congruent.*

Timmy connected what he had learned to the world around him. He wrote: *Imagineing how much shapes in the world would be imposable. There would be at least 30 shapes on one piece of property. And my little house proply has 10,000,000 shapes, I think? I wonder who invented the names for shapes?*

Jenny explained how she changed her mind about mathematics: *I used to think that math was tortcher, but this year, because of the geometry menu, geometry to me is a fun part of math.*

What I Learned From the Geometry Menu

I learned some very interesting geometry words, like: concave, convex, quadrilaterel, perpendicular and so on. I found 5 stratagies for "Square-Up." I learned the names of a: 7 sided shape heptagon, a 9 sided shape nonagon, and a 10 sided shape decagon. I found out that a square is a special kind of rectangle. I used to think that math was ~~tortcher~~, but this year, because of the geometry menu, geometry to me is a fun part of math.

Jenny was specific about what she had learned—and about how her attitude toward mathematics had changed. (Grade 3)

Lisa wrote about her confusion with math: *When I first started 3rd grade I got realy mixed up with geometry and mathematics and I still do get a little mixed up with math and geometry but not so much. I learned: 1. Many shapes can be turned into other shapes with only moving one piece. 2. Math isn't just for adults. 3. Math can be fun. 4. I never knew a diamond can be called a rhombus. 5. never to give up. 6. you need a key two open a locked door.*

Sara was extremely enthusiastic about the unit. (Grade 3)

What I learned from the geometry menu

I learned so much! Shapes. geometry. I really liked Rotating Shap.es. I dicocoved that shapes are fun, shapes are so, so, so fun. I also dicocovered in rotating shapes that when you do a shape over and over new shapes start to a pear. I love how new shapes apear. I looks like afishal math. I+ really does. I also learned that four tryangles makes other shapes. Yes. I used to think four tryangles only made a tryangle. That was befor I came in this class ofcourse.

In square up I learned so many difernt ways to make a square. This last menu we just had was my faverit so far. Yes it was.

CHAPTER 7

Creative Writing and Math

From time to time, I try to give a writing assignment in math class that is more like a creative writing assignment, such as asking students to write stories or poems that relate to what we're studying. I give these assignments for several reasons. First, an assignment that calls for a fanciful approach can give students a fresh way to think about mathematical ideas. Second, students who feel they are more interested in writing than in mathematics, or are more confident about their writing ability, can bring their strength to a math assignment. Third, an assignment like this can help students broaden their view of mathematics.

Math Haiku (Grade 3)

Each year, Dee Uyeda teaches her third grade students in Mill Valley, California, about Haiku poetry and has them write Haiku about all subjects. Her students write and illustrate their poems.

Nick's Haiku captured the importance of zero.

These Haiku were written
by third graders.

Infinity

Please stop,

I want to talk to you.

Circle:

No sides

No corners.

Math

In a book

Just sits.

Metric Measuring (Grades 3–4 and 6)

I taught a measurement lesson on metric units of length to a class of third and fourth grade students. To give the children concrete references for 1 centimeter, 10 centimeters, and 1 meter, I gave each of them a white Cuisenaire rod, an orange Cuiseniare rod, and a length of string that was 1 meter long. I posted three charts and labeled them "1 cm," "10 cm or 1 dm," and "1 m." I asked the students to find things in the room that were the same length as the white rod, orange rod, and string, then record what they found. As well as introducing the children to metric units of length, the activity gave me the opportunity to talk about the approximate nature of measurement. We talked about why "a little bit off" with the 1-meter string wasn't as much a problem as "a little bit off" with the 1-centimeter rod.

After the activity, I gave the students the assignment of writing stories entitled "If I Were One Centimeter High." The assignment gave them the chance to think about the measurement of 1 centimeter in relation to objects in the world around them and to exercise their imaginations. The children enjoyed writing the stories and reading them aloud to the class.

If I was one Centemeter High.

If I was one cm. high I would be called a shrimp because everyone would be one dm. high or one meter high! I would be so small that no one could see me! My sister would be 5 cm. high + my mom would be 20 cm high + my dad would be 30 cm. All my friends would be 2, 3 or 4 cm. high! I was the smallest person in the world and I ran away because everyone was calling me a shrimp! The End

Susan worried about being called a shrimp. (Grade 4)

If I were one centimeter high....

I could walk in the grass and it would look like a jungle. I would fight with the ants and when I got in trouble with them. I would hop on a butterfly's back and fly away. When I fell off its back I wouldn't hurt myself. I would land in a TV repair shop and I would help the man repair it. When his cat chased after me, I would run into a mouse hole. I wouldn't come out till late at night, when everone was asleep. Then I would hicthhike crickets to my house and go to sleep a nice soft cottenball.

Derek's vivid imagination emerged in his story. (Grade 4)

iF I were one centimeter
I Live in a ball oF chocolate
the size of the sun It would
be hollow and I'd Live in
it all my LiFe and There
Would Be No school to go
to and No one would Be
Poor and OFcourse milk to go
with the chocolate and No one
could get cavaties or sick
not even a cold and
evry one Would live For a
millon years and Pools Would
Be Filed with chocolate

Rusty described an idyllic life as 1 centimeter tall. (Grade 3)

I did the same exploratory activity with the white rod, orange rod, and string with sixth graders who had not yet been introduced to metric measures of length, and I asked them to write stories about being 1 centimeter tall. They also enjoyed the assignment, and I collected their stories into a book that they shared with other classes.

Vivian wrote her story as a bad dream. (Grade 6)

If I Were a Centimeter High

One day as I was walking into my house I suddenly looked down and I was about one centimeter high. I looked up and I saw my dog. I yelled and screamed but nobody could hear me. I ran over to my mom and jumped on her shoe. She didn't feel a thing so I climbed her pants and it was not as easy as I thought it would be.

I climbed her shirt and then I took hold of her hair and as I thought she screamed and shook her head and I fell off and bumped my head and I was asleep for three hours and when I woke up I was my normal size.

Alex's story involved his entire family. (Grade 6)

If I Was One Centimeter Tall

Suddenly, I awoke to find my self of a different size. It seemed to me that my bed was 1,000 times bigger then it was before. I climbed out of my bed and slid down the edge. To my surprise I found the whole family the same size as me. "Hi dad" said John.

We managed to live like this for two days. We then decided that this was to much so we decided to live out in the open, but Jenney did not agree and suggested that we live in her doll house and we all agreed.

Suddenly the whole family grew to their normal size except me. So I always had to watch out that nobody would step on me.

One day I walked into a toy store and grabbed a car and drove off into the street and I almost got ran over but I drove down a gutter.

I managed to survive the rest of my life like this.

If I was a Centimeter High

I'm a centimeter high. You see, when I was only two years old I had some kind of liquid pored on me. Of course it was an accident, but it sure was a bad one.

There are many disadvantages to being so small. For instance, I don't go out in public very often because I get trampled. If I do go out in public, I usually go out in my mom's pocket or purse.

At night I sleep in a walnut shell filled with cotton. And of course I have some blankets too. It is very comfortable. My old room is our guest room. I sleep on my mom's nighstand.

One day my mom was vacuuming. I was sitting down watching tv. (which seemed like the screen in a movie theater to

me) when suddenly the mouth of the vacuum came dangerously close me. I jumped out of the way in the nick of time. Then my mom vacuumed up my bed! Oh boy!

"Mom, Mom," I cried, but she didn't hear me. Later that day she made me a new bed. Then she said that I had to be in another room when she was vacuuming.

I like being a centimeter tall in some ways. I hope some day I might be a little taller though.

Julie described how she nearly had a disaster being so small. (Grade 6)

Tangram Stories (Grade 2)

In a unit on geometry, I read to the class the children's book *Grandfather Tang's Story* by Ann Tompert. In the book, Grandfather Tang tells the story of two foxes that change into other animals to outdo each other. One changes into a rabbit and the other into a dog, the rabbit turns into a squirrel and the dog into a hawk, and so on. With each animal, Grandfather Tang creates a matching tangram shape.

After reading the books, I distributed tangram puzzles and had the children explore making the various shapes. Then I suggested to the children that they write stories of their own. Using some of the illustrations from the book, they invented their own situations, and they wrote and illustrated their stories for their class library.

Kelly wrote an involved story that she titled *Irving and Fluffy*. She wrote: *Once their was an old man. He loved to run around. His name was Irving. He was very poor but he had his cat Fluffy. Irving and Fluffy always play every day but one day Fluffy ran away. Irving tried to find him but he could not find him. He cried and then he said, "I will change into a bird and look for him." Then he spotted him and the cat said, "I will change into a tree and then he will not know it's me." So he changed into a tree. Irving did not know where he was so he said, "I will change into a dog and find him." So he changed into a dog. He sniffed the tree that was Fluffy and Irving said, "I found you Fluffy" and started to scratch the tree. So Fluffy said, "I'll change into a snake and crawl away." So he changed into a snake. Irving saw the tree shrink but he didn't see Fluffy change into a snake. So he said, "I'll change into . . . " and he saw Fluffy his normal self and Fluffy said, "Take me home" and he looked around and he saw Irving running and the cat said, "Hey, wait up" and the cat started to run.*

Daniel used a good deal of descriptive words in his story: *Once there were two wolves. They liked to hunt everyday. Their names were Diego and Adam. But one day they were in a fight. "I'm more powerful than you are," said Adam. "I am more powerful than you are," said Diego.*

"I can turn into a dog faster than you can," said Adam. Adam changed into a dog with a blink of Diego's eye.

Diego turned into a mouse in a flash. Adam turned into a cat. Adam tried to get Diego, but he was just too fast. So Adam turned into a snake. This time Adam new he was going to win. But Diego turned into an eagle and started to dive after Adam. Adam stormed across the field slivering as fast as he could. Diego kept on going.

Adam turned into a lizard. Diego new that he could not cetch him now. Diego gave up and turned back into a wolf. So did Adam.

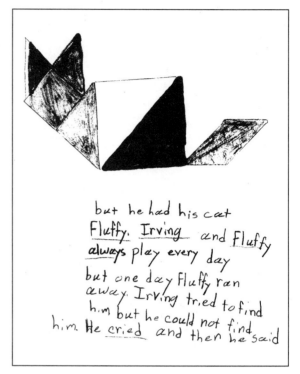

Once there was
an old man.
He loved to
run around.

His name was Irving

He was very poor

but he had his cat
Fluffy. Irving and Fluffy
always play every day
but one day Fluffy ran
away. Irving tried to find
him but he could not find
him. He cried and then he said

These are two of the seven pages in Kelly's story. (Grade 2)

The Two Wolves

Written and
Illustrated by
Daniel

This was the cover for Daniel's story. (Grade 2)

General Writing Assignments

From time to time, I give writing assignments that don't focus on students' understanding of mathematics but on an aspect of their mathematical learning. Although students sometimes include information in journal entries or other papers about how they feel about their learning, I find that when I ask them explicitly about an issue, I get a general view of the class as well as insights into individuals.

Over the last several years, I've given a variety of these kinds of assignments. One is to have children write about mathematics in general or about what were their most and least favorite activities in a unit and explain why. Another is for students to write about how they worked with their partner or group on an activity or during a unit, or to write in general about working cooperatively. Sometimes I have students write the directions for an activity or game they learned in class so that they can teach it to someone at home. I've also had students write letters to introduce classroom visitors to the kinds of things we do during math time. I keep these letters in a folder so that visitors have something to read that gives them a general introduction to our math program. Sometimes, at the end of the year, I ask students to reflect on what they've learned. All of these assignments are useful windows into how students respond to their learning experiences.

The Importance of Mathematics (Grades 2, 5, and 8)

I'm always concerned that students see the significance of what they're learning in school, and I try as much as possible to help them see why math is important for them to learn. One way that helps me address this is to hear their ideas, either about mathematics in general or about some specific topic.

In one second grade class, I asked the students to write about why math is important. I wrote a prompt on the board:

Math is important because _____.

Elena's thoughts were practical. She wrote: *Math is important because if you do not paye the bills you coud be on the streets because you haf to figur out everything. There are lots of Math problems and you haf to add up all the taxis and you haf to be a problem solver.*

Timmy's paper showed his struggle with writing. He wrote: *Math is inportont bokus in kalag* [college] *I wod have to do lots of math thas why its inportont.*

Timmy's view of why math is important pointed toward his college education. (Grade 2)

> Math is inportont bokus in
> kalaG I Wod have to do lots
> Of Math thas why its in
> portont.

In her paper, Grace looked to the future. She wrote: *Math is important because if you are a grown-up you might want to have a store of your <u>own</u> and if they give you cash what will you do if you didn't no math?*

Grace's paper addressed how math can be important to adults. (Grade 2)

> Math is important because if you are
> a grown-up you might want to have a
> store of your own and if they give
> your cash what will you do if you
> didn't no math?

Molly also wrote about stores but with a somber twist. She wrote: *If you are at a store you havf to now abot math and if we didn't have math we wudent have stores and if we dindint have stores wed diy.*

Andrew had a broader view. He wrote: *Becuse anything you do has math in it. Math is important becase evan if you are making a car you will be using math. Money is math. Math is important because all your life youll be doing math.*

As I often do with assignments, I had volunteers read their papers aloud, and we talked about all the different reasons why it's important to learn about math.

Cheri Schuricht had her fifth grade students in Edmonds, Washington, write about why math is important. Most of them thought about the value of math for their future.

For example, Keri wrote: *I think math is very important. I think it is important becauase we use it all the time. We might not notice it, but we do. Parents use math in their businesses, and kids use math in school. Some doctors need math if they work in a pharmacy. My dad needs math because he's an insurance broker. My mom needs math because she's a travel agent and needs to figure out BONUS MILES. Math is also important because if we didn't have it, what would we do?*

Karim wrote: *Math is important because you have to use it for your whole life. You use math the most in school unless you have a job as an engineer or teacher. All people need math to do daily work. Even when you play professional football you have to under stand numbers so you can spend your money.*

> Why Math is important
>
> The reason math is important is that when you get to be an adult you have to know mathematics so you can get a job and to know or not know what to get at the grocery store.

Seth wrote about why math is important. (Grade 5)

Joan Carlson also had her eighth grade students in Mendocino, California, write about the importance of mathematics. Like the fifth graders, most of the eighth graders focused on the usefulness of math in their future.

Why Math is Important

Math is important because many people use math in their jobs. For instance my mom is a bookeeper at a ▓▓▓▓ restaraunt. She counts money, fivres the budget, and figures the profit. My dad is in excavation he digs trenches and leach lines, and holes for septic tanks. He needs to know the grade of the land, how much fall and how many hours he worked so he knows how much to get paid.

You also need math in playing pool because you have to know what angle to shoot at so it will go into the write hole.

Without math everyone would suffer.

Antonio wrote about how his parents used math in their jobs and also about how math can help when playing pool. (Grade 8)

Krissy explained her view that "we would still be in the dark ages" if we didn't have mathematics. (Grade 8)

Just imagine your at your new job. You work for a fast food restraunt and your a cashier. If you don't know your math you could give out too much money or recive too much (not a bad idea). Even at this job math is critical! It is the same thing if you are an accountant. If you don't know your math (which you should if you got in this profesion) you could get into all sorts of problems. Math is used every day, country, and throughout the world. If math wasn't here today we would still be in the dark ages.

Even though most of the population dislikes math, they should reconize it once in a while because it is very important!

Writing About Partners (Grade 3)

One year I randomly assigned third graders a different partner for each unit and had them write each time about how they worked with their partner. "Try and write things that give your partner feedback about how he or she worked well," I said. "If you have some criticism, try and write about it in a way that could help your partner improve."

After the students wrote, I had them exchange their papers with their partners and then talk about what they learned. I kept the tone positive. "Remember," I said, "your job is to try and help one another become better learners."

The students in some pairs had similar views of each other. For the multiplication unit, the third unit that year, Joel and Josh were partners. Josh was exceptionally gifted numerically, and he enjoyed thinking about numbers in his head. He felt good about himself as a math student. Joel struggled with academics in general. He was interested in sports, excelled at playing them, and was popular with many of the boys. Josh also enjoyed sports, and he and Joel were friends.

Joel wrote: *Me and Josh worked good he helped me with the work alot and I yous't to think I wasin't very good it math but Josh helped me with it. And I'm better in math now.*

Josh wrote: *Joel and I worked good together. Joel usually did the writting and Joel and I both did the thinking though I did a little more of the thinking but the days I was sick Joel did all the work so it's about even.*

Joel and Josh had similar views about each other as partners. (Grade 3)

James and Sally had a rocky experience as partners. James was an unusual boy, a unique and often profound thinker, with a wry sense of humor. He was interested in a wide variety of subjects, including ancient Greece, habits of bugs, and plays. Sally had two older sisters who were having social and academic difficulties in high school, and Sally was often absent. When she came to school, she was often too tired to participate. James wrote: *Sally was not a good partner at the begining. I rated her 1.7. Avg to me is 4.3. When Sally got back we had a big fight but she got in a better mood. I rated her a 3.9 then. At the end I rated her 4.3½. thats all.*

Sally wrote: *At first James was very anoying. But after awhile it was sort of entrasting working with James. I started to lern a lot from James so now I understand math a lot more. He did somethings and so did I.*

Sometimes, partners did not hold similar opinions. For example, Lisa wrote: *Lydia and I worked well together, I think we traded off being the thinker. Most of the time, I did the thinking and Lydia did the writing.* However, her partner wrote: *I worked with Lisa. I would not want to work with her again. She always tells me what to do.* Lisa was generally more comfortable with adults than with children, and she often remained aloof from the other students. Given the choice, she preferred to work alone, unless an adult was available. Lydia was a shy, quiet, and easygoing girl who got along well with others. Lisa was surprised and a bit hurt by Lydia's feedback, and I talked with her about how her behavior contributed to Lydia's reaction. Addressing problems like this is one of the responsibilities of teaching, and having children write, even in math class, can provide useful insights and information.

What Makes a Good Partner? (Grades 4, 7, 8)

Joanne Lewin had her fourth graders in San Francisco, California, write about what makes a good partner.

Michael focused on the benefits of having a good partner. He wrote: *I am gonna talk about how to be a good partner.*

It's Wonderful to have a good partner because he/she will help you on anything your in trouble on. I like best of a good partner is the he/she could talk to you, help you and organize you. Good partners can work with you and help you on anything you need help on. He/she will listen to you and shares ideas to you.

That's what it takes to be a good partner.

Rebecca felt she had learned a good deal about working with partners and had specific suggestions. She wrote: *In Ms. Lewin's fourth grade class* we work with partners a lot. So I have learned what it takes to be a good partner. You get more ideas as a partner becaus there are two people thinking about the same thing.

To be a good partner you need to listen to other peoples ideas and consider what they say. You need to split up the work and help your partner. You need to talk clearly and quietly and not put your partner down. You need to stay with your partner and not go talk to someone elce. And not be bossy and do all the work but still be down to business.

Jonah also included specific suggestions in his paper. He wrote: *I am going to talk about how to be a good partner.*

A good partner works with you and helps the other one. Some of the things that help is that he could give you ideas, helps you spell and catch mistakes or things like that. A good partner will cooperate with you and shares ideas with you. He or she shouldn't fool around or we won't get done.

I hope I can be a good partner and my partners are good too.

Jonah offered tips about how to be a good partner. (Grade 4)

In his paper, Nathan gave advice about how to be a good partner. He wrote: *Being a good partner is very importnat because it's something you will need for the rest of your life.*

To be a good partner you have to listen well and participate and cooperate with the person you're working with. If you don't do these things the other person ends up doing all the work, and if that happens nobody will want to work with you.

My idea of a good partner is someone that is willing to help you and do half the work, and discus the problem.

People have to work at it to become a good partner. That's what I think it takes to be a good partner.

Although Chiung preferred to work by herself, she gave specific advice about how to be a good partner. (Grade 4)

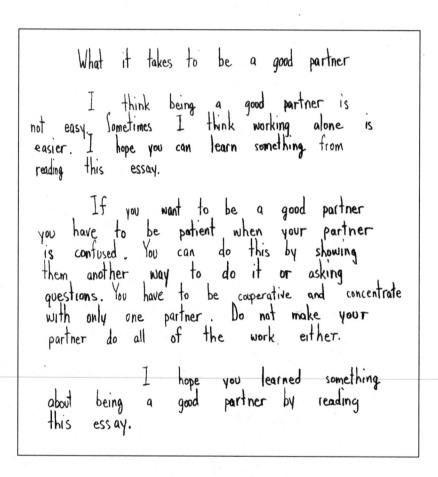

What it takes to be a good partner

I think being a good partner is not easy. Sometimes I think working alone is easier. I hope you can learn something from reading this essay.

If you want to be a good partner you have to be patient when your partner is confused. You can do this by showing them another way to do it or asking questions. You have to be cooperative and concentrate with only one partner. Do not make your partner do all of the work either.

I hope you learned something about being a good partner by reading this essay.

When I asked a class of seventh graders to write about being a good partner, I received a variety of responses. Polly, for example, included in her paper: *You have to listen and not be too bossy and not make your partner feel dumb.* Polly's comment seemed to relate directly to the problem she had working with Sean. Sean is a quick thinker who often is impatient with others who do not think as quickly. He found it difficult working with Polly.

In his paper, Sean wrote: *Working with a partner really can help both people. Because people can do different things and in a partnership the person who can do it best can lead the way. But the other person has to do his/her share too and not be a slouch. When one person is a slouch the other person can get mad and then no good work gets done. Each person has to pull his/her weight.*

Andy's paper revealed the benefits he saw about having a partner. He wrote: *I think taking turns and sharing the work load helps a lot. Like when you have to write, you can let one person do it for one activity, and then the other goes. That way it's not so bad. I think it's good to have a partner because there's allways someone there to help you. A good partner should be someone who helps.*

Joan Carlson asked her eighth grade students in Mendocino, California, to write their thoughts about what was needed to be a good partner or group member. Although the students expressed their views differently, all of their papers hinted at the need to be helpful, patient, positive, and willing to do your share.

For example, Lenny wrote: *A good partner in a group is a person who listens to what other people have to say. They are courtious to the other group members and they try to work out problems without arguing with each other. When you work in a group, everybody has to contribute an equal share. That is what makes a working group.*

Nadia wrote: *You have to work together. You have to be able to go with the flow, not argue and always want to be in the spotlight. Don't get me wrong. It's good to want to be a leader. However, sometimes you need to let others "rule the roost". You have to be understanding. Sometimes people make mistakes, & you need to be there to help, not to hinder. You can't expect to always have your answer be the only one that's "right". People other than you can think to. Don't be worried about if you can write more or less, or get done faster or slower. Everyone has there own pace. Just take time to do a good job. Basically, your group is a tiny clan; everyone person has to be there own job, pull their own weight. Sometimes even more.*

Rebecca listed her advice. She wrote:

1. Be nice to all group and class members. Do not gang up and be cruel to any certain person.

2. Just because their not your friend does not mean you can't be nice to them.

3. If your having more trouble than you can handle by yourself ask the teacher, he/she can help you.

4. Pay close attention to what the teacher tells you, it's most likely to be important.

Sean's comments were brief. He wrote: *I think that it takes the willingness to work and do your part and to help others. You also shouldn't let your partner do all the work. Share the burden.*

What it takes to be a good
Partner

One of the most important things about working with another person is to be careful not to take over more than half the work.

This is very hard to do because you can get carried away in the middle of a project and leave your Partner in the dust. If this happens I sometimes think of something extra to do for them, but most often I feel guilty that I am doing their work for them.

Other qualities that make a Group member are Communicational Skills as well as problem solving and logic.

Henry's paper revealed his concern about taking over too much of the work. (Grade 8)

The Benefits of Working in Groups (Grade 8)

Cathy Humphreys asked eighth graders in Palo Alto, California, to write about how working with others helped them in math class.

Ruth's paper expressed the ideas found in many other students' papers. She wrote: *I think working with others helps me because you can ask people in your group for help if you need it. Sometimes classmates can explain certain things better than the teacher. Also, if you didn't understand about the instructions, you can ask your group members to help explain any misunderstandings. Another thing is they can help you find where you possibly made a mistake. So, I personally like working with others.*

A few students pointed out possible disadvantages. Kerry, for example, wrote: *Sometimes it helps a lot to work in a group because other people may think of things you wouldn't think of, or a different way to solve a problem. One time, somebody pointed out that their answer was different than mine. When I checked over it, my answer was wrong.*

Working together can also be bad, because sometimes only 1 or 2 people do the work and the other people just copy or sit there. Usually, it depends who you're with.

Part 3
TIPS AND SUGGESTIONS

As with many new experiences, the process of incorporating writing into math teaching may involve growing pains, both for teachers and for students. My skill and comfort with making writing an integral part of math instruction have evolved over years of experience in which I've made many mistakes and discoveries. From trial and error, I've learned a great deal about how to encourage children to write, and my teaching techniques have improved.

Also, I've seen improvement in students' ability to write about mathematics and in their willingness to write in math class. Over a school year, writing in math class seems to change for students from a tag-on demand to math assignments, to a reasonable extension of what they're doing in class, and finally to a natural and integral part of their math learning.

The writing students do in math class, however, differs in several ways from much of the writing they do for language arts assignments. Their math writing is typically not creative writing, and having a final product suitable for publication isn't the goal. Rather, what they write in math class is a way for students to reflect on their learning and communicate their ideas about mathematics. In this section, I offer tips and suggestions for helping students write in math class.

Establishing Purpose and Audience

When Saul Bellow was asked for his thoughts about the Palestinian uprising on the West Bank and Gaza Strip, he replied, "I don't know. I haven't written about it yet." His response may have been a quip or a dodge, but it embodies the basic purpose of having students write in math class. Writing helps students sort out, clarify, and define their thinking.

Frustrated with a writing assignment in math period, Matt, a sixth grader, blurted out, "Why do we have to write, anyway?" His question surprised me into attention. The raised heads of his classmates indicated that he had their attention as well.

This was after just a few writing assignments in math period and early in my experience with writing in math class. While the purposes and benefits of having children write were becoming clear to me, I had never talked with the class about my thoughts.

"That's such an important question," I responded. "Let me tell you why I ask you to write." My mind was swirling. I realized that I had not clearly explained to myself the reasons for their writing and that my own thoughts had not jelled. I felt it was important to respond, but didn't feel well prepared to be coherent and convincing.

"When I went to college, I knew I wanted to become a teacher," I remember saying. "In my sophomore year, I decided to become a math teacher. This wasn't because I liked math best; there were other subjects that interested me as well. But I didn't enjoy writing. While assignments in most classes required writing papers, math assignments required only doing problems. I guess I chose math because I was lazy."

I could tell this rambling wasn't very enlightening or interesting to Matt or to the other students, but I was searching. I pressed on, feeling somewhat confessional.

"Advanced math courses got increasingly more difficult for me. I was able to write formulas with fancy mathematical symbols and signs, but I didn't always understand what I was doing. More and more, I relied on figuring out how to solve problems by following examples in the textbooks. Often, I didn't understand why the examples made sense. My teachers couldn't tell from my homework what I was thinking. They could only see the math symbols I wrote on my paper, not the confusion in my mind.

"Now that I'm a teacher, I feel that when you hand in assignments, I need to understand what you're thinking. Otherwise you could be in the same pickle as I was—not understanding—and I might never know. So I ask you to write so I can learn about your thinking."

My answer wasn't particularly interesting or satisfactory to the students. I'd seen that glaze on their eyes before. Nor was my answer satisfactory to me. It served the purpose of getting the students back to work, but I was disturbed.

Two years later, I was questioned again by a student, this time by Gabe, a third grader. Gabe expressed his frustration differently.

"I don't want to write," he announced when I gave an assignment. I was surprised and challenged by this, but this time my response didn't have the apologetic tone I had felt with Matt and the sixth graders. I felt stronger, clearer, and better prepared. The two years of additional experience had helped me. My response was more energetic.

"Let me tell you why I ask you to write," I said to Gabe. The others at his table listened as well. "My job is to help you understand math. To do my job, I need to know what you do understand and what you don't understand."

I rested my hand lightly on his head and continued. "I sometimes wish I could just lift the top off your head and look inside and say, 'Oh, so that's what Gabe is thinking.'" The children giggled at this.

"But I can't do that," I continued. "So I ask you to write to explain what you are thinking. When I read what you write, I learn about what you understand."

Gabe was satisfied. And I was satisfied with my response. Also, I learned another lesson from this. I was reminded that it's important for students to understand what they're being asked to do in class. They need to hear why I feel it's important to make writing part of their math assignments. It's essential to talk with the class about this at the outset and not wait for the question to arise.

Gabe might still raise his question, even after I've given what I thought was a clear explanation of the importance of students' writing in math class. That's okay; he has a right to ask as many times as he wonders about it. Now I welcome the question. It gives me an opportunity to talk with the students about what I value. It gives me a reason to reinforce what I've told them, to present my thoughts in a new light, to help them understand, and to give them encouragement.

As my confidence and conviction grew, I began to raise the issue with classes rather than waiting for them to do so. In a unit with sixth graders about the area of circles, students were working in pairs to find the area of a circle using six different methods. I wanted them to write about each method, describing what they did, why the method made mathematical sense, and how they felt about its accuracy. I had spent most of the first period giving directions for each method. In the last 15 minutes of the class, the students got to work.

Before the students returned to work on the second day, I talked with them about the writing requirement of their assignment. "I read a book last summer titled *Writing to Learn*, written by William Zinsser. The book gave me a great deal to think about, and one quote from the book has stuck in my mind—'Writing is a way to work yourself into a subject and make it your own.'"

I read the quote again and then asked, "What do you think Mr. Zinsser meant when he wrote that?" Several of the students had ideas to share.

"When you write something down in your own words, then you really understand it," Chris said.

"Your own words belong to you," Keky said, "and they're your ideas and no one can change them."

"You have to think about something before you can explain what you think when you write," Meghan said.

"When you have to write something," Nate offered, "then you have to organize your thoughts. You can't just write something down; you have to think it through."

"I don't know how to say this," Amir began, "but when you have to write, first you have to figure out what you're going to write or else you can't write it."

"Writing forces you to think," Michael said.

After all of the students who wanted to offer their ideas had had a chance to do so, I told the class that I had another reason for having them write. "Not only does writing help you think about the math we're study-ing," I said, "it helps me as a teacher. When we have a class discussion, not everyone has the chance to say something. But it's important for me to know what each of you is thinking, and your writing gives me insights into your ideas. So I'd like the recording you do to be as thorough and thoughtful as you can make it."

Too often, the rationale for what we do in the classroom isn't obvious to students, and students don't have access to the information. We as teachers must clarify the reasons for our instructional choices and find ways to make them clear to students so they are informed and motivated.

Helping Students Write

Students typically need a great deal of guidance and support to become comfortable writing in math class. Especially at the beginning of the year, I provide students with clear structures for writing assignments and give them as much encouragement as I can. The amount of structure and support I continue to offer during the year depends on the progress of the particular students. With all classes, however, throughout the year I reinforce the purposes of writing, set structures for assignments, and offer encouragement.

One structure that I provide is that when I give a writing assignment, I give students titles for their papers and prompts that they can choose to use to begin their writing. For example, when I give students a problem to solve, I name the problem for them to use as a title and might write on the board:

> I think the answer is _____.
> I think this because _____.

Sometimes I give prompts that are specific to a particular assignment. For example, at the beginning of a unit on multiplication, I asked third graders to figure out how many chopsticks we would need for the 28 people in our class. I wrote on the board:

> The Chopstick Problem
> We need ___ chopsticks.
> I figured it out by _____.

I don't demand that students use the prompts I offer. What's important to me is that the students' writing relates to the problem and makes sense, not that it follow a particular form.

Karin was one of the few third graders to use the prompt I provided for the chopstick problem. She wrote: *We need 56 chopsticks. I <u>figured</u> it out by adding: 2 + 2 + 2 + 2 + 2 + 2 + 2 + 2 + 2 + 2 + 2 + 2 + 2 + 2 + 2 + 2 + 2 + 2 + 2 + 2 + 2 + 2 + 2 + 2 + 2 + 2 + 2 + 2 = 56. I think the problem was pretty easy. But, I did not enjoy doing the problem.* When I asked Karin why she didn't enjoy the problem, she answered, "There were too many 2s and I goofed up." Her paper showed how she had to erase the extra 2s she wrote.

Karin used the prompt to write her solution to the chopstick problem. (Grade 3)

Most of the other students expressed their answers in other ways. Kim, for example, wrote: *We need 56 chopsticks. Because if you gave everyone one chopstick that would Be 28 chopsticks. Then you give everyone one more chopstick and that would be 56 because 28 + 28 is 56.*

Paul wrote: *I figured out that we need 56 chopsticks by adding 20 + 20 and then adding 8 + 8 and that adid* [added] *up to 56.*

The prompt I provided was not necessary for these two students. They both presented solutions and clearly explained how they reasoned.

When I give directions for a writing assignment, I typically end with the same reminder. "Use words, numbers, and, if you like, pictures to explain your thinking," I say. I realized how often I give these directions when Eugene blurted out one day in an exasperated tone, "You always say that." The rest of the class giggled. "Well, it must be important to me," I mused aloud.

The Chopstick Problem

We need 56 chopsticks. Because if you gave everyone one chopstick that would Be 28 chopsticks. Then you give everyone one more chopstick and that would be 56 because 28+28 is 56.

$$\begin{array}{r} 28 \\ +28 \\ \hline 56 \end{array}$$

The Chopstick Problem

We need 56 chopsticks.

I did it like this.

$$\begin{array}{r} 28 \\ +28 \\ \hline 56 \end{array}$$

but there is another way to do it,

2+2+2+2+2+2+2+2+2+2+2 +2+2+2+2+2+2+2+2+2+2+ 2+2+2+2+2+2.

but $\begin{array}{r} 28 \\ +28 \\ \hline \end{array}$

is eseyer.

Although neither of these two solutions used the prompt I gave, both students answered the problem. (Grade 3)

When I circulate in class as students write, they often ask for help. "I'm stuck," they'll say, or "I don't know what to write." In those instances, I talk with them. First, I ask them to describe the assignment. I might ask, "Explain the problem to me" or "What do you have to do on this assignment?" or "Tell me what you're supposed to write about." Students' responses to my queries help me see whether or not they understand the assignment.

Then I try to elicit some of their ideas. Depending on the assignment, I might say, "Do you have any idea about what the answer is?" followed by "Why do you think that?" Or I might say, "What ideas do you have?" or "Tell me something you know." I probe to get them talking. When a student offers an idea, I say something like, "See if you can say those words again in your head and then write them down on your paper."

Sometimes this still doesn't help, and some students remain puzzled about how to begin. At these times, I've explained that they should push the words they've said back through their mouths up to their brains and then let them go again. "This time," I say, tracing a path on my own body, "let the words go right past your mouth and travel into your shoulder, down your arm, through your hand, and out your pencil onto the paper." It sounds corny, but the description is graphic, and it seems to give some children a new way to think about getting their ideas down on paper.

I've come to learn the importance of having children talk about their ideas before they write—in a class discussion, in a conversation with a small group, or with another student. Talking is easier than writing for most children, and students write more thoughtfully and fluidly when they've had the opportunity to verbalize their thinking aloud before tackling a writing assignment. Having students talk in class discussions is especially helpful because they can hear other ideas and points of view. I also reinforce for the students that writing about someone else's idea is fine, as long as the idea makes sense to them and what they write explains how it makes sense.

Of course, there are times when you've had a class discussion, set a clear structure for an assignment, and still students feel that they don't understand the assignment or don't know what to write. What to do in these instances depends, of course, on the students and the situation.

If I notice that the problem exists with more than one student, I'll interrupt the class and ask who would like to meet and talk about the assignment some more before they begin. If the problem is with only one student, I'll try and work with him or her myself, or ask, "Who in the class do you think could help you get started on this assignment?" and pair them up. I try a variety of methods, just as I do in any situation where a student doesn't understand and I need to provide additional assistance.

There are days when a student just can't do an assignment. Sometimes I'll ask a student to write about why he or she is having difficulty, even if it's only one sentence. I might say to the student, "The more information you can give me, the better I'll be able to think about ways to help you understand."

Challenges such as these are part of teaching in general, not specific to having students write in math class. There's no one right or best way to deal with these situations. I rely on talking with students, exploring new ways to help them interact with the mathematics, and searching for different ways to encourage them to write.

How Long Ago Was 1976? (Grade 3)

This lesson was one of many that helped me realize the benefit of preceding a writing assignment with a class discussion. Before reading a book to third graders, I told them that the book had been written in 1976. "How long ago was that?" I asked. It was then 1989. I asked the children to think about how they might figure out the answer.

After a few moments, I asked for volunteers to report their ideas. Sam explained how he started from 1977, counted on his fingers to 1989, and came up with 13 years. Angie, however, reported that she started counting at 1976, and got 14. She showed us what she did, using her fingers as Sam had to keep track as she counted. I noted puzzled looks on the faces of some students about the different answers. I decided not to comment at this time but, instead, to hear from other students. I called on Jason.

"I know it was 13 years ago," Jason said emphatically. "My sister was born in 1976 and she's 13 years old." Others laughed, and Jason grinned, enjoying the attention.

Joshua, who was adept at dealing with numbers in his head, also arrived at 13, but he had a different approach. He explained, "You add 10 to 1976 and that gets you to 1986, and then you count 3 more to get to 1989."

"Mine is kind of like Joshua's, but different," Lisa said. "I added 4 to 1976 and that got me to 1980. Then I added 10 more, but that got me to 1990, so I had to come back 1. I think it's 13."

Eli was impressed by Lisa's idea. "Oooh, that's neat," he commented.

Rebecca, however, was confused. "I don't get it," she said.

Tanya had a different idea. "I think you should subtract," she said, "but I don't know how to do it in my head."

After about 15 minutes of discussion, I asked the children to write about the problem. "You can explain how you figured in your head," I said. "Or use paper and pencil or a calculator, as long as you can explain your reasoning." I also reminded them that they could present their own idea or someone else's idea.

"What you write has to make sense to you," I added, "and help me understand how you reasoned."

This writing assignment went particularly well. I think that because of the discussion, the students had ideas from which to draw and, therefore, were confident about tackling the assignment. They understood the assignment, had some way to approach their writing, and eagerly went to work.

> I figgyerd ouT 13 because you have 1976 + 4 = 1980 then I added 10 and I had four teen. and took away one and got 13 1989

Lisa's idea had impressed Eli and he used it in his paper. (Grade 3)

Karin used Jason's idea of relating the problem to someone's age. (Grade 3)

> My sister is 13 and I think that my sister was born in 1976. So, it's easy! 13 years.

When I reviewed the students papers, I found that half of the class had counted on to get their answer, some getting 13 and the others thinking the answer was 14. This made for a lively discussion the next day. Except for Tanya, none of the students connected the situation to a subtraction problem! This helped me realize that the children needed to experience many different kinds of situations that relate to subtraction.

> it was thirteen years ago because if you put 1976 and count up 1977 1978 1979 1980 1981 1982 1983 1984 1985 1986 1987 1988 1989
> 1 2 3 4 5 6 7 8 9 10 11 12 13

Brandon figured by counting up from 1977 to 1989. (Grade 3)

> It was 13 years ago because I counted like Melina did (76) 77 78 79 80 81 82 83 84 85 86 87 88 89! Thats how I did it! Well it could be 14 if he wrote it at the beginning of the year.

Laura, always the peacemaker, tried to justify how 13 and 14 might both be possible answers. (Grade 3)

Strategies for Addition Facts (Grade 2)

This lesson also went particularly well. I think this was not only because of the discussion we had, but also because I modeled on the board some ways to write about the ideas the students presented. I taught this lesson to second graders. I wanted to focus them on basic addition facts, not by having them memorize answers but by helping them think about ways to figure out sums.

To begin class, I wrote on the board:

$$5 + 1$$

I asked the students to raise their hands if they thought this was an easy sum to figure out. Practically all the students raised their hands.

"Why is it so easy?" I asked.

"I just know it," Tomo said.

"Because you just start with 5 and go 1 more," Timmy added.

I then wrote *1 + 5* on the board.

"What about this one?" I asked.

"It's just as easy," Catherine said, "because you just turn it around."

"Why does turning it around make it easy?" I asked.

"Because," she answered, "if you do it the other way, then you have to count too much. You have to go 1 . . . 2, 3, 4, 5, 6." She used her fingers to show.

"So, you have a way that helps you," I said. Catherine nodded. I wrote on the board:

Start with the larger number.

I then wrote *5 + 6* on the board.

"That's easy," Jason said. "You do 5 plus 5 and then you go 1 more."

"Why is that easy?" I asked.

"Because I know 5 plus 5," he answered.

"Is 5 plus 5 easy for everyone?" I asked. There was general consensus. I wrote other doubles on the board—4 + 4, 3 + 3, 6 + 6, and so on—and asked the class to say the sums in unison.

"So the doubles are easy," I said, writing Jason's suggestion underneath Catherine's:

Go to a double that's near.

"I just remember them," Sophia volunteered.

"That's another strategy," I said, using the word for the first time. I wrote *Strategies* to title the list, and added Sophia's idea:

Just remember it.

"What about this one?" I said, and wrote *9 + 8* on the board.

I waited a few moments to give the students time to think, and then I called on Seth. "It's 17," he said, "because 9 plus 9 is 18 and then you go down 1 to 17."

"How do you know that 9 plus 9 is 18?" I asked. Seth shrugged.

"I know!" Michael called out. Seth looked relieved, and I asked Michael to explain.

"Because 10 and 10 is 20," he said, "and you have to take 1 off each 10, so you take 2 off the 20 and that leaves 18."

I then pointed to the problem on the board and asked if anyone had a different way to add 9 and 8. Ryan and Leslie offered their ideas. Each was the same as Seth's. Emily said she had a different way.

"You start with the 9 and count up 8 more," she said.

"Yes," I said, "I've seen many of you count." I added Emily's strategy to the list, even though it was similar to the first one I had written. Emily was often shy about sharing her ideas, and I wanted to acknowledge her contribution. The list now looked like this:

Strategies
Start with the larger number.
Go to a double that's near.
Just remember it.
Start with the larger and count on.

I then wrote *6 + 7* on the board. "This time, I'd like each of you to write down all the different ways you could figure out the sum," I said.

"How many ways do we have to write?" Michael asked.

"At least three," I said, "and more if you can."

The discussion and writing on the board had prepared the students for this assignment, and all but one were able to explain at least three ways to find the sum.

Each of these students described five different ways to figure out 6 + 7. (Grade 2)

$6 + 7 = 13$

Stradegies for Addition

1. Count, 1, 2, 3, 4, 5, Ect. Ect.
2. Take doable 6 + 6 = 12 and add one (=13)
3. "Remember!"
4. Take 4 from 7 and add to six It = 10. Add leftover 3 it = 13! Yay!
5. Start with ten and count on the rest.

Srategies for Addition
6+7

① 6+6=12 and at one more is (13).

② 7+7=14 and one less is (13).

③ You have 7 and you count on a (to 6) 1,2,3,4,5,
6, = (13)

④ You have 6 and you count on a (to 7) 1,2,3,4,5
6,7, [13]

⑤ 5+5=10 + 3 = (13)   When you
add   5+5   You have 1
leftovre   in   6   and 2
leftovre   7   1+2=3   thats
(13)

Strategies for Addition
6 + 7 = 13

① 6+4 is 10 so It is 6+4+3=13
② You do like this 6, 7, 8, 9, 10, 11, 12, 13.
③ 6+8 is 14 14-1 is 13
④ 6+6=12 and then you add 1 more
⑤ All you got to do is count your fingers
or look at them.

Color Tile Riddles (Grade 8)

Not all lessons go as smoothly as those described on pages 134–139. For example, I ran into problems during four days at the beginning of one school year when I had eighth graders solve and create riddles with Color Tiles. The activity engaged the students in making conjectures, testing conjectures, and evaluating the ideas of others. Writing had not been a part of these students' experience and, for the most part, their instructional program hadn't pushed them to think and reason. The students were more comfortable being told what to do and learning how to do it.

To prepare for the activity, I labeled two paper bags *Riddle 1* and *Riddle 2*, put Color Tiles into each one, and wrote clues for each bag to describe its contents.

I began the lesson on the first day by presenting the clues for riddle 1. I wrote the clues on the board one by one, each time asking the students to show with Color Tiles what might be in the bag. After five clues, the students were able to identify that there were six blue and three yellow tiles in the bag. The five clues were:

> Clue 1. There are fewer than 15 tiles.
> Clue 2. I used two colors.
> Clue 3. There are no green or red tiles.
> Clue 4. I have twice as many blue tiles as yellow tiles.
> Clue 5. There are three more blues than yellows.

For the rest of the period, I repeated the activity using the other riddle I had prepared.

For the second day, my plan was to have the students work in pairs to write riddles of their own. To prepare them, I held a class discussion to hear some of their ideas about writing clues. I planned to write some of their ideas on the board to clarify how they might get started with this assignment.

"If you were going to make up a riddle like the ones I presented yesterday," I asked, "what might you do to get started?" As students volunteered, I recorded their suggestions on the board:

> 1. Put some tiles in the bag.
> 2. Write a clue that gives information but doesn't give it away.
> 3. Write more clues.
> 4. Test the clues to be sure they produce exactly one solution.

I then gave the students directions about how they were to proceed. "You'll work in pairs," I said, and gave each pair a paper bag and Color Tiles. I suggested that they follow the steps on the board.

"Use no more than 15 tiles," I said, "and write your names on the paper bag as well as on your paper."

As they worked, many students needed reassurance that the first clues they wrote were okay. When students asked me to, I read their clues and either told them that their clues made sense to me or gave them feedback to help them rethink their ideas.

Other students had trouble even getting started, often due as much to some disagreement with their partners as to a lack of clarity about what to do. If it were a partner problem, I mediated; if they weren't sure what to do, I reviewed the clues I had introduced the day before and suggested that they pattern their clues on the ones I had presented.

When I read clues, I found that many of them had grammatical errors. In this instance, I asked the student to read his or her clues aloud. Often this made the error evident either to the student reading the clue or to the partner. If not, I pointed out the error and talked with the students about correcting it.

I was busy during this lesson. Although the assignment was mathematically within the reach of the students, it required that they generate ideas and write them down, and this differed from the worksheet assignments they were accustomed to doing.

#1 We have less than 15
#2 We have one more green than red.
#3 Green is an even number
#4 We have 4 colors.
#5 We have more than 12
#6 There is only one tile for one color
#7 There are the same amount of blues as yellows.

Sinead and Krystal's clues led to one solution. (Grade 8)

1) I have more than 3 and less than 14
2) I have all four colors
3) I have three times as many reds as yellow
4) I have more blues than reds and more reds than yellow
5) I have the same amount of greens and blues

Halbert and Robert had to add a fifth clue to make their riddle work. (Grade 8)

All of the students completed their riddles during class, and I reviewed them that night. I noticed that some of the riddles had redundant clues, and some led to more than one possible collection of tiles. To focus on these problems, I began class on the third day by presenting a new riddle. I wrote five clues on the board:

1. I have fewer than 15 tiles.
2. I have three colors.
3. I have twice as many yellow tiles as blue tiles.
4. There are two colors with the same number of tiles.
5. I have the same number of yellow and red tiles.

After working on these clues, the students realized that there were two possible solutions—two red, two yellow, and one blue tile and four red, four yellow, and two blue tiles. I told the students that I had put four red, four yellow, and two blue tiles in the bag and asked them to suggest additional clues that would produce this answer.

"You could say that you had more than 5 tiles," Krystal suggested.

"You could write that you used 10 tiles," Andy said.

"It could say you have between 6 and 12 tiles," Robert offered.

I wrote their ideas on the board and acknowledged that each of these clues would work.

Then I asked, "Which clues that I wrote weren't necessary?" This was more difficult for the students to analyze. After some discussion, there was agreement that clues 2 and 4 could be eliminated.

"Clues that aren't necessary are called redundant," I said.

I then gave directions for solving their riddles. I explained that I had stapled each of their riddles to their bag of tiles. "That way you can check your answer when you've solved a riddle," I said.

I also explained their writing assignment. "Describe how you figured out the solution," I said. "Include your thoughts about what clues were most helpful, what confusion you experienced, and what clues you feel could be improved." I wrote these points on the board.

"Also," I added, "list the clues you think could be eliminated and explain why." After I gave them some procedural directions about having me check their work before they chose another riddle to solve, the students got to work.

All of the students got involved and enjoyed the assignment, but many had difficulty writing explanations. For example, although most students were able to identify the redundant clues, most did not attempt to explain why they were unnecessary. "I don't know what to write" was a common response when I questioned the students. And when I'd probe and ask how they knew a clue was redundant, I received answers such as "You can just tell," "It's too hard to explain," or "I just know." Again, I was busy during the class, troubleshooting, encouraging, and managing.

Solution 8G 4R 2y 1B

☑ Too Easy, ☐ Just Right, ☐ Too Hard

Explanation

Clue 3, 4, and 5 works. First I got one of each color, then then I put twice as many yellow as blue then twice as many green than red. Then I subtracted 1034-1019. Then I put out 8 green.

Redundant

Clue 1 was redundant "We have all the colors" because of clue 3 "I have twice as many yellow as blue and twice as many green as red" clue 2 was redundant "We have more than one tile"

Solution
4 green, 3 yellow, 2 blue and 1 red

☐ TOO EASY ☒ JUST RIGHT ☐ TOO HARD

EXPLANATION: 8+3+5 helped.
We just went through all the clues and it worked out very well.
None of the clues could be improved. None at all.

Redundant Clues —
Number 2 you could have done without.

Students solved one another's riddles and explained what they thought about the clues. (Grade 8)

For homework that night, I asked the students to write clues for a collection of one red, one blue, three green, and six yellow tiles. The next day, I arranged the students in small groups and asked them to compare their riddles. Near the end of class, I explained their next homework assignment, which was to write a letter to me about their experience with Color Tile riddles. I wrote on the board several questions that they should address in their letters:

Did you enjoy the activity? Why or why not?
What math skills did you use?
Would you recommend I teach this to other classes? Why?
What suggestions for improving the lesson can you offer?

I gave the students time in class to begin their writing. Again, I was busy answering their questions about setting up their letters, how to get started, if what they wrote was all right. Although there seemed to be fewer questions, many of the students were still uneasy.

Improvement with writing assignments comes over time. I planned to continue to give these students additional experiences in class explaining their reasoning and further assignments to write about their thinking.

Having students write letters gives insights into their views about what they study. (Grade 8)

Dear Ms. Burns

I think the thing your doing with the color tiles is good because your teaching different types of math in a fun way. When we first started out doing it I thought it would be hard but now that I'm use to it and know how to do it I like it and I do recommend you do it with other classes. There is nothing wrong with the way you do it but you should add more color and make it more interesting.

Dear Mr. Burns,

I enjoyed your project on the chips. It not only made us solve problems but make them too, and I like doing that.

In the project I mostly used deduction until you came to the last number.

Yes I recommend you do this with other classes I'm sure they would enjoy it because it's different then what is usualy taught in a math class.

I have no suggestions for improvement to offer you

Andy answered each question in a separate paragraph. (Grade 8)

The Benefits of Cooperative Learning

When students work, discuss, and write together, they have more opportunities to verbalize their thoughts, get reactions from others to their thinking, and hear other points of view. Listening to other students' ideas can help those who don't understand gain new perspectives on the topic. Explaining their reasoning can help students who do understand to cement and even extend their understanding. All students benefit.

Having students work cooperatively reduces the isolation of working alone and gives individuals support for taking intellectual risks. When working in pairs or small groups, students get instant feedback on their thinking in settings that are safer than whole class discussions. Working in small groups can encourage otherwise shy or hesitant students to talk, which helps them clarify their ideas and prepare for writing.

Writing assignments can incorporate cooperation in several ways. At times, students can collaborate on a writing assignment and produce one paper. At other times, students can work cooperatively on a problem but write individually, so that all students have the opportunity to explain their thinking with their own words. Deciding whether students should work together or not, or write collaboratively or not, should depend on the purpose of the assignment. What's important is that students understand the rationale for how they are to work.

A Measurement Problem (Grades 6 and 7)

I learn a great deal from lessons that don't go well. As difficult as they are, lessons that are problematic usually push me to think more about my teaching practice. In this case, my lesson with sixth graders helped me realize that when students work alone, they often lack the support that would help them learn.

For the lesson, I planned to have the students work individually to solve a measurement problem involving fractions. Before the period began, I drew on the chalkboard a line segment that measured $22\frac{1}{2}$ inches. (The students didn't know the length of the line segment.) Also, I put 33 Unifix cubes into a plastic bag.

"When I snap these cubes together," I said, "do you think the train will be longer, shorter, or about the same length as the line segment I drew?" The students had no way of making a reasonable prediction by looking at the bag of cubes, but they were willing to guess.

After all who wanted to had voiced an opinion, I asked, "How could we find out?"

"Do it!" they answered in unison.

Two students snapped the cubes together. They matched the train to the line segment and found that the train was about 2 inches longer than the line segment. We discussed what "about the same length" means when measuring. We had a lively conversation about when it was necessary to be accurate (building shelves for a bookcase, measuring fabric for a dress, or timing a soft-boiled egg) and when approximations would suffice (cutting paper and ribbon to wrap a gift, measuring water for cooking spaghetti, or dishing out equal portions of mashed potatoes).

Then I asked them to make a different estimate. "How long do you think the line segment is?" I asked.

"It's shorter than the yardstick," Mark said. The yardstick was resting on the chalkboard tray.

"Maybe 30 inches," Marcie said.

"How many cubes long is it?" Peter asked. Peter's question led us in the direction I had planned.

I held the train up to the line segment and removed three cubes so that their lengths matched. Then I split the train into 10s. There were 30 cubes in all.

"So the line segment is as long as a train of 30 cubes," I said. "Can that information help you figure out the length of the line segment?"

"How big are the cubes?" Amy asked.

"They're $\frac{3}{4}$ of an inch on each side," I said. "What else do you need to know?"

There were no more questions. I then said, "I'd like you to figure out how long the line segment is. When you record your answer, be sure to explain why it makes sense." The students got to work.

The room became quiet with the kind of quiet that test taking often produces. Some students started to write about their ideas; some did calculations on their papers; others gazed into the distance, apparently thinking. As I watched them, I noticed that the students seemed lethargic in contrast to their liveliness during our discussion about measurement.

The students' papers gave me much to think about. Scott's paper was representative of many of the students who couldn't make any headway. He wrote: *I have not figured this out because I don't know how. I'm stuck!*

Some students made some progress, but ran into snags. Jonathan, for example, wrote: $\frac{3}{4} \times 30 = \frac{37}{4} = 9\frac{1}{4}$ *First I multiplied $\frac{3}{4} \times 30$. I think this is a good way of doing this because all you have to do is multiply the numbers and you have your answer.* Jonathan didn't look at the line segment on the chalkboard to notice that an answer of less than 10 inches made no sense.

Karine came up with an interesting beginning. She wrote: *I know its less than 30 inches because the cubes are smaller than 1 inch. Its more than 15 because that would be half and $\frac{3}{4}$ is more.* She was then stumped and had no place to turn.

Mark made a good start but then took a false turn. He wrote: *Two cubes make $1\frac{1}{2}$ inch. 4 cubes make 3 inches. So 8×3 makes 24 inches.*

Jessica was one of three students for whom the problem was easy, even trivial. She wrote: *$22\frac{1}{2}$ I multiplied $\frac{3}{4} \times 30$. 30 is equal to $\frac{30}{1}$. I multiplied and then I reduced to get my anwer. It makes sense because you're doing $\frac{3}{4}$ 30 times. It's easy to multiply it.*

What I had done was put the students in a testing situation, not a learning situation. Dealing with fractions is difficult for many students, and they need as much support as possible to learn about them. By having students struggle individually, I didn't provide any way for them to get feedback on their thinking or hear about other students' approaches. And when they are working individually, there's no way that I can get around to help all of them.

Cathy Humphreys presented the same problem to seventh graders. She introduced it as I had. However, rather than have the students solve the problem and write individually, she had them work in groups of four. That way, the students could talk with one another and draw from their collective thinking.

To promote further communication in the class, Cathy gave each group an overhead transparency and marker. "Record your solutions and your thinking on the transparency," she said. "Then each group will present its thinking."

The groups' interactions were animated and their explanations revealed that the students used a variety of approaches. Group 6 wrote: *22½ because we know that each cube equals ¾ inches. We rounded ¾ to 1 whole inch. Then we multiply 30, because there is 30 cubes by 1, which equals to 30. We drew ten sticks. 1 inch equals to ⁴⁄₄ and so we need ¼ more to make 1 inch. Four of ¼ = 1 inch out of 10 sticks it equals to 2½. If we do that for 3 times it equals to 7½. We subtract 30 by 7½ which equals to 22½.*

Group 3, however, used both decimals and fractions to figure out the problem. They wrote: *1.00 = ⁴⁄₄ so ¾ = .75 so we multiplied .75 × 30 = 22.5 which is 22½ inches. Our answer is 22½ inches. Another way we figured it out was 30 × 3 ÷ 4 = 22.5.*

Group 6 figured the length of the train if the cubes were 1 inch long, and then adjusted. (Grade 7)

Group 3 used a combination of fractions and decimals. (Grade 7)

Group 1 wrote: *The total inches are 22.5. We think its 22.5 because each cube is ¾ of an inch and their is 30 cubes so you split one each into 4 parts and you times 30 cubes by 3. And you get 90. And then divide 90 by 4.* They showed how they did the calculation.

Group 7 had a different approach. They wrote: *The answer is 22½. Our group figured it out by putting two cubes together. Two cubes = 1½ inches. Then we multiplied 1½ by 15 because we used 2 cubes to make 1½ we cut 30 in half which = 15. That's how we got our answer.*

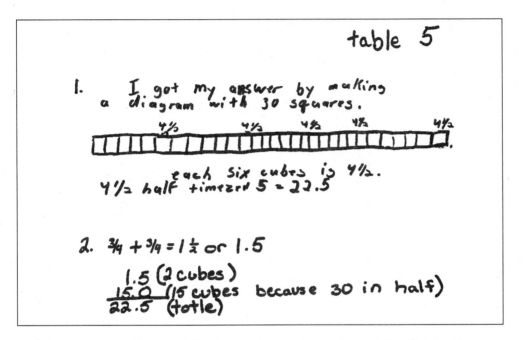

Group 5 gave two solutions, first figuring the length of six cubes and then figuring the length of two cubes. (Grade 7)

Counting Fish (Revisited) (Grade 2)

When I posed the problem to second graders of figuring out how many "fish" there were after 25 children and 4 adults each put two cubes in a bowl, I allowed the children to choose whether they would work in pairs or alone. (For details about the complete lesson, see pages 17–20.) I had intended for the students to work individually on this problem. But before I explained this, Andrew raised a question.

"Is this a partner or individual problem?" he asked.

Before I could answer, several children gave their opinions.

"Make it partners," Nick said.

"I think we should work together," Jonathan said.

Several other students had opinions as well. It was clearly an issue about which many of them had strong feelings. I called them back to attention and told them I was interested in their ideas. I had planned to have them work individually, but I was willing to hear their thoughts, and I was interested in their ideas.

"But you can't call out," I said. "Raise your hand if you want to tell your idea." More than half the class wanted to talk, and I gave all who wanted a turn the chance to speak.

"I think we should work together," Grace said, "because you don't waste time that way."

"It's funner if you have a partner," Rudy said.

"It's better if you do it together," Timmy said, "because you can talk and get help if you need it."

"I like to work alone," Andrew said, "because when I work with some-one, I just tell the answer, and they don't always believe me." Andrew's math ability surpassed his communication skills.

"I don't have a partner," Molly said. Amelia was absent. "Seth doesn't have one either because Abby isn't here. Can I go sit with Seth?"

"Does that mean you'd rather work with Seth than alone?" I asked. She nodded yes.

"I think we should do it in partners," Leslie said, but she had no reason to offer.

"It's better to work in partners," Nick said, "because you don't have to do all the writing yourself."

As they were talking, I was thinking about what to do. Teaching often requires making decisions on the spot, and it's hard to give an idea careful consideration in the midst of a lesson. Generally, I have children work individually when I'm particularly interested in checking on their individual abilities. However, I also know that when they're working in pairs I have a chance to assess as I observe and listen to them talk among themselves. I decided that in this case it really didn't matter. I was interested in information about each child's understanding of the 10s and 1s structure of our number system, and I planned to use this activity to assess their understanding, but this part of the lesson was just the introduction to the assessment I'd planned. I collected my thoughts and made a decision.

"Let me tell you how we'll work," I said, and waited for them to quiet down and give me their attention. "There actually are two parts to this problem. I know for sure that I want you to do the second part individual-ly because it will give me information that will help me know more about your thinking. But, for the first question, it's okay with me if you work alone or with a partner. So it's your choice."

After giving the children a moment to think about how they would work, I gave further directions. "When I come to your table, tell me whether you're going to work alone or with a partner. If you're working alone, I'll give you your own sheet of paper. If you're working with a part-ner, I'll give you one sheet for both of you to use."

Of the 25 students, only 4 decided to work alone. There were nine pairs and one group of 3. I felt good about how this evolved. I want to support children taking charge of their learning as much as possible. Also, I was interested in their ideas about working alone or with partners and was curious to see the mode each student chose.

It turned out that the two students who had expressed a desire to work alone, Grace and Andrew, wound up working with partners; Maria, who had wanted to work with a partner, chose to work alone.

Working Together or Alone (Grades 3 and 5)

At times in other classes, when children were working together on a group assignment, a child has asked if he or she can write an individual report instead. For example, when teaching a unit on division, I gave third graders the following problem: Four children were walking to school together one day. They found a sack that was full of marbles. They brought the sack to their teacher who suggested they give it to the principal, as whoever lost it would most likely check in the office. The children did so. A week later, the principal called the four children into the office and said that no one had claimed the marbles. She told them they could have it, but that they would have to share the marbles equally. The children counted and found there were 54 marbles in all.

"How many marbles should they each get?" I asked the children. "Work in your groups to solve the problem and write one paper that explains how you did it."

Groups solved the problem in different ways. One group, for example, counted out 54 Unifix cubes and shared them. Another group figured out that if they each took 10 marbles, there would be 14 left, and then they would each get 3 more with 2 remaining.

> We had 54. We gave each person 10 Because we thout IF there was 40 there would be 4 tens and 14 would be left. Each person gets 3 witch leves 2. Each person get 13.

Shaney, Nick, and Gabe started with what they knew—dividing 40 by 4—and then dealt with the rest of the marbles. (Grade 3)

This group used trial and error and addition to solve the problem. (Grade 3)

Each person should get thirteen marbles. The way we found this out is because we added thirteen four times and two one time.

```
  13              1          12
  13             14          12
  13             14           2
  13             14          12
 ___             14         ___
  52            +14          48
+  2           ____
 ___             56
  54
```

As the class was working, Jill came up and asked me if she could write her own paper. I asked her why.

"I can't get them to understand my idea," she said, "and I want to write it down. I think I have a good way to do it." Jill seemed excited about her idea. She wanted to write about it while it was fresh, and this seemed fine to me.

At another time, a fifth grader, Marcie, said to me, "I don't want to write with my group." When I asked her why, she told me she couldn't work with the others. Rather than allow Marcie to work individually, I chose to talk to the group about their problem and help them resolve their difficulty so they could work together. Marcie's request stemmed from her social difficulty, not from her interest in another intellectual pursuit, so I decided to try and help her learn to work with her group.

Many situations in the classroom require instant decisions, and many of them are surprises that test our professional practices. Although we can plan lessons, we can't prepare for everything that might occur during those lessons. In these two instances, the instructional goals I had, coupled with what I knew about Jill and Marcie, were factored into my decisions. But still, my decisions were examples of the judgment calls that teaching regularly demands.

For examples of student writing about working in groups, see Chapter 8, pages 113–123.

I wrote down 54, I took away 12, I got 42. I took anther 12 away. I got 30. I took another 12 away. I got 18. I took another 12 away. I got 6. Then. I took away 4, I got 2. ~~then I took away~~ ~~4 there were 4 left I got~~ I chiped each of them into halfs that made 4 halfs. Each pearson got 13 and a half.

Jill saw the problem differently than the others in her group and wrote an individual solution. (Grade 3)

Using Students' Writing

As often as possible, I incorporate students' writing into classroom instruction by presenting ideas from their papers and using them as springboards for class discussions and activities. This not only reinforces for students that I value their writing but also helps them see how their ideas can contribute to our classroom learning. Also, they receive recognition for having their ideas benefit the entire class.

Sometimes I ask students to read their papers aloud. That way, while one student revisits his or her own ideas, the others hear another point of view. I choose papers that offer the potential to lead to further discussion of a mathematical idea we're studying. I don't necessarily choose perfect papers, but I'm careful not to use papers that would embarrass a child or point to his or her lack of understanding.

High or Low (Grade 3)

During a probability unit with third graders, Andrew became interested in whether high sums or low sums were more likely to come up when two dice were rolled. To find out, he invented a game and wrote about it in his log.

In Andrew's game, one player took the low sums, from 2 to 6, and the other took the high sums, from 8 to 12. Neither took 7, so each player had five sums. Players took turns rolling two dice. They recorded the sum that came up on each roll and continued to play until one sum had come up 12 times. The winner was the player who had that sum. Andrew had played the game several times with Timmy, and he was convinced that the higher sums were more likely to win.

A few days later, I asked Andrew to present his game to the class so that everyone could enter into the investigation. After a lively discussion about Andrew's conjecture that high sums were more likely to win, the students paired up and tried the game. We collected data about which sums won and the number of times high and low sums came up.

Which Number Wins?

29   11   38

2	3	4	5	6	7	8	9	10	11	12
1+1	2+1	1+3	2+3	4+2	4+3	2+6	6+3	6+4	6+5	6+6
		1+3	3+2	3+3	6+1	4+4	5+4	6+4	6+5	
		3+1	3+2	3+3	5+2	5+3	5+4	6+4	6+5	
		3+1	3+2	4+2	1+6	2+6	5+4	5+5		
		3+1	3+2	1+5	5+2	5+3	5+4	5+5		
			3+2	5+1	6+1	5+3	6+3	6+4		
			4+1	3+3	4+3	6+2	5+4	6+4		
			3+2	4+2	6+1	6+2	6+3	5+5		
			3+2	4+2	4+3	5+3	6+3	5+5		
			4+1	5+1	6+1	4+4	5+4	6+4		
				5+1	5+2	6+2	5+4	5+4		
						6+2				

To play Andrew's game, the students rolled two dice and kept track of the sums that came up. (Grade 3)

When all the students had had a chance to play and think about the game, I asked them to write about whether they thought high or low sums were more likely to win, or whether they thought the chance was the same. The students' papers revealed a mixture of clear thinking, uncertainty, partial understanding, and some confusion.

There were 25 students present that day, and 12 of them wrote about why they thought high sums and low sums were equally likely. Leslie, for example, wrote: *I think 2–6 and 8–12 are equally likely because they all have same cominations like 12 and 2 have only 1 combination and 5 and 9 have only 4 combinations. So it doesn't really matter which one you root for.*

> ## Which Number Wins? – Andrew's Version
>
> I think 2–6 and 8–12 are equally likely because they all have same cominations like 12 and 2 have only 1 conibination and 5 and 9 have only 4 Combinations. So it doesn't really matter which one you root For.

Leslie explained why she thought high sums and low sums were equally likely. (Grade 3)

Eight students wrote about why they thought high numbers would win. Andrew based his reasoning on data the class had collected. He wrote: *I think the high numbers (8–12) are more likely because I added up all the games and higher numbers had 571. Lower numbers had 474 and 7 had 207. The higher numbers had 97 more rolls then lower numbers and had 364 more rolls then 7. All together we rolled 1252 times.*

I think there is a reason that the higher numbers are winning but I don't know what it is.

> ## Which Number Wins –
> ### Andrews version (me)
>
> I think the high numbers (8~1. are more likely becacese I added up all the games and higher numbers had 571. Lower numbers had 474 and 7 had 207. The higher numbers had 97 more rolls then lower numbers and had 364 more rolls then 7. All together we called 1262 times.
> I think there is a reason that the higher numbers are winning but I don't know what it is.

Andrew wrote about why he thought higher sums were more probable. (Grade 3)

Teddy didn't have a reason for thinking that higher sums were more likely; he felt he needed more data. He wrote: *I think that the hier numbers would win but I can not explane why. I am going to have to play this game a lot more to find out if the hier numbers or the lower numbers is better.*

Using the game Andrew had written about in his log for a class investigation not only acknowledged his contribution but also gave the message to the rest of the students that I paid attention to what they wrote in their journals and valued their ideas.

Dividing into Groups (Grade 3)

During a unit on division, Lynne Zolli talked with her third graders in San Francisco, California, about the different reasons she organized them into groups. Lynne then asked, "If we put all 28 students in our class into groups of 2, 3, 4, 5, 6, 7, 8, 9, and 10, how many groups would we have each time?" The students solved the problem in various ways, and Lynne used their papers to discuss their different approaches.

Reggie listed multiples to figure out how many groups there would be. (Grade 3)

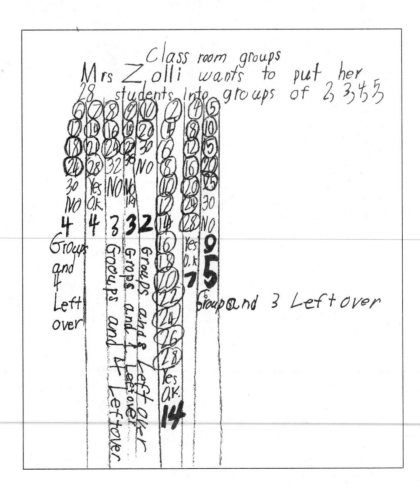

Reggie, for example, listed the multiples of each number and then circled each one stopping at 28, if it was on the list, or at the largest multiple that was less than 28.

Gabrielle divided 28 by 2 to figure out the number of groups with 2 in each. To do the division, she first divided 20 by 2, then divided 8 by 2, and finally added the two answers to get 14. For the other problems, she drew 28 circles for each, arranging them into groups of 3, 4, 5, and so on.

After dividing 28 by 2 numerically, Gabrielle solved the rest of the problems by arranging circles into groups of 3, 4, 5, and so on. (Grade 3)

Wesley also drew circles and used a method of counting to determine how many there were in each group.

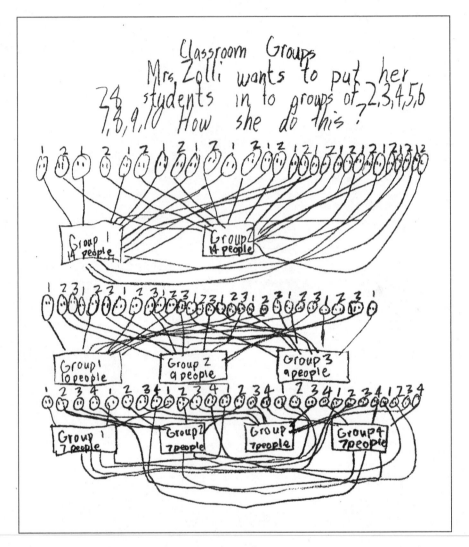

Wesley drew circles, but used them in a different way than Gabrielle did. (Grade 3)

Truc used multiplication, calculating in his head how close he could get to 28 for each grouping and then figuring the remainders.

In a class discussion, Lynne used the students' work to discuss the different approaches possible for thinking about division, and how division relates to multiplication. When a discussion about an idea such as division comes from the work students have done, from their own thinking and experience, mathematics becomes more relevant to them.

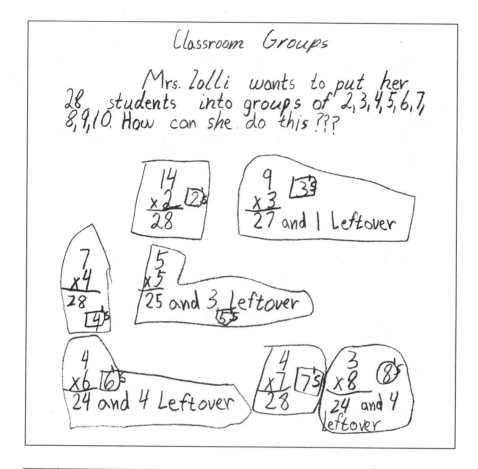

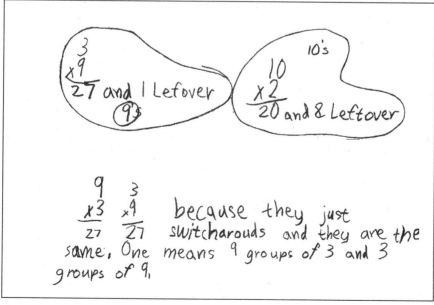

Truc's solutions showed his understanding of the relationship between multiplication and division. (Grade 3)

My Travels with Gulliver (Grade 5)

When I taught a unit based on the book *Gulliver's Travels*, fifth grade students learned about measurement, estimation, ratio, proportion, area, and perimeter. (See the Bibliography on page 193.) For one activity, I assembled a collection of common objects and asked the students to choose one and make a life-size tracing of how big the object would be in Brobdingnag, the land of giants. The objects included postage stamps, pennies, marking pens, playing cards, chewing gum wrappers, paper clips, calculators, toothpicks, and earrings.

The students had compared heights in previous activities. I had shown them the length of a "glumgluff," a unit of measure in Lilliput, and they had noticed that it was as long as the side of a Snap cube—about ¾ of an inch. They figured the height in our units of the king of Lilliput, who was 8½ glumgluffs tall. Later in the unit, they were introduced to a 9-year-old girl from Brobdingnag who was almost 40 feet tall and ascertained that objects in Brobdingnag were about 12 times taller than objects in our world. The students were able to compare lengths, such as people's heights or how tall steps were, but I was curious what they would do when thinking about how to enlarge two-dimensional objects.

The students who chose to enlarge a penny approached the problem in several different ways. Jeremy began with the circumference of the penny.

Jeremy used the circumference of a penny to enlarge it. (Grade 5)

> A Brob life-Size Tracing
>
> The Penny. I got a string and put it around the penny. Then I timesed it by 12 and got my answer. (look on back)
>
> I made a lasso and put it around the penny then I cut the lasso off and measured it then I timesed it by twelve.

He wrote: *The Penny. I got a string and put it around the penny. Then I timesed it by 12 and got my answer. (look on back)* Jeremy had fashioned the string, which was 12 times as long as the circumference of a penny, into a circle and taped it on the back of his paper. Then he wrote more to explain what he had done: *I made a lasso and put it around the penny then I cut the lasso off and measured it then I timesed it by twelve.*

Daria noticed that the diameter of the penny was the same length as the side of a Snap cube. She wrote: *I measured a penny and it's one glumdgluff, so I took twelve glumdigluff cubes and put it around in a form of a circle 6 times and came up with this.* What Daria had done was snap together a train of 12 cubes and use the length of the train as the diameter for a penny in Brobdingnag, positioning it six times until she could trace a circle. Her drawing of a penny was larger than Jeremy's string circle.

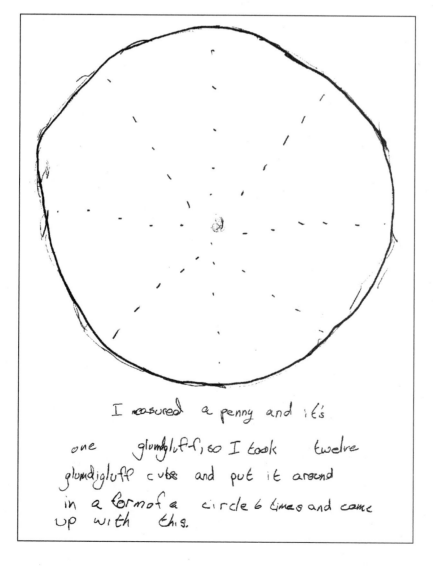

Daria measured the diameter of a penny and made a Brob penny with a diameter 12 times longer. (Grade 5)

Cary tried a different approach. She took 12 pennies and clustered them together to fashion a shape as close to a circle as possible. Then she traced a circle around them. Before she wrote about it, however, Cary noticed that other students were making much larger pennies for Brobdingnag, so she abandoned her idea and decided to enlarge the toothpick instead.

Nick took another approach. He traced a penny onto ¼-inch graph paper and noticed it was three squares across. In the center of his paper, he drew a square that approximated the size of the penny, three squares by three squares. He knew he had to make it 12 times larger, and counted 12 of the graph-paper squares up, down, and to the sides of the square he had drawn, and traced a circle. He knew something was wrong with his method. He wrote: *I used this graph paper (and many others) to find how big a penny is in Brob. I placed a penny in the square and counted up down to the sides. I checked with other poeple who did this and found out it is to small. The real size is bigger than this paper.* Nick was stuck and did not know what else to do.

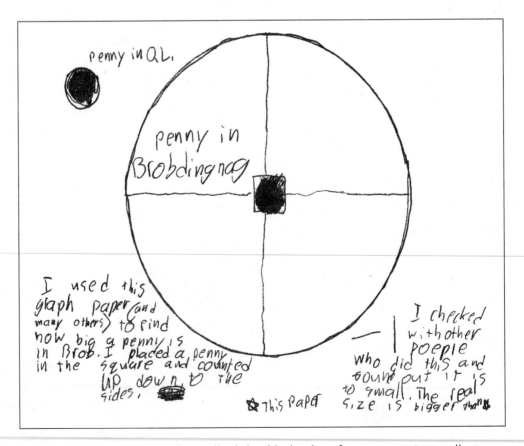

Nick used the ¼-inch squares, but realized that his drawing of a penny was too small.
(Grade 5)

A few days later, I presented these four different methods to the class. At first, most students thought that all of the approaches made sense. But when they saw the different size circles, they realized that something was wrong. Now, they were all stuck.

I talked with the students about what they had learned about the 40-foot girl. We had drawn one of her hands and realized that not only did we have to make it 12 times longer than ours, but also 12 times wider.

"Or else it won't look right," Courtney had observed. "It would be too long and skinny."

Jonah noticed that it would take more than 12 of his handprints to cover the enlarged hand.

"Lots more," Gabe commented.

After discussion and investigation, the students realized that 144 of our handprints would cover the area of a hand in Brobdingnag. They also realized that a penny in Brobdingnag would have to be pretty big to "look right" in a Brob hand.

"I bet you'd need 144 pennies!" Lauren exclaimed.

From using the ideas they had written about, all of the students were introduced to thinking about how areas of shapes grow when their dimensions are increased.

Giving Feedback

I read students' writing for clarity and completeness and try to give feedback that is encouraging, substantive, honest, and specific. I avoid comments that are merely praise, such as "Good work" or "Excellent." I don't grade their work. Instead, I give feedback on the substance of what they've written. If I find their mathematical thinking unique or interesting, I tell them that and explain why. If I find their writing lacking or confusing, I tell them that as well.

When I read students' papers, I write notes when I have comments to make, usually on Post-its. Sometimes I use students' papers in class discussions to help students see different approaches and learn more about what is acceptable to me. During these discussions I sometimes encourage students to give feedback to other students about their papers.

Students working on assignments during class often bring me their work, either when it's in progress or when they think they're finished, and I discuss it with them. When young children bring their papers to me, if possible, I have them read the papers aloud.

I ask students to revise their work when their papers do not give complete or detailed information about their thinking. This happens a great deal of the time. When I feel they need to explain more, I often say, "That's a good beginning," and give some guidance. "I need to know more about how you reached that answer," I might add, or "Write some more about why you're sure that idea is correct," or "Add some details or examples to help me better understand your idea."

Sometimes, depending on the child, the assignment, and the moment, I ask students to edit their work and make spelling and grammatical corrections. I have a general class policy that the children should underline words they don't think they've spelled correctly. Then I can give them feedback, either assuring them that the spelling is correct or giving them the correct spelling.

I find it's helpful to post in the room lists of words that relate to the mathematics the class is studying. At the beginning of the school year, I make a list of the names of the manipulative materials we use, including their colors and shapes. Also, I post a list of the different areas of math we'll be studying—number, geometry, measurement, probability, and so on. Then, as we study each new area, I start an additional list for vocabulary that directly relates to it.

I have no rule that I always follow about having children make corrections. Sometimes when children misspell words that are on one of the charts, I refer to the chart so they can compare and correct their spelling; sometimes I just give them the correct spelling and ask that they make the correction; sometimes I accept a paper with errors. Similarly, when children bring papers to me without punctuation, sometimes I ask them to read their papers and add periods and capital letters; sometimes I don't. These decisions depend on the child, the words, and the situation, and I consider making decisions such as these as part of the craft of teaching.

Using Students' Writing as Models (Grade 5)

For a first writing assignment with a class of fifth graders, I decided to have them do an activity and then describe what they did. I felt this writing would be fairly straightforward, as they would be writing from their direct experiences. The activity I chose was for each student to figure the area in square centimeters of one of his or her feet. We were beginning a unit on area and perimeter, and I decided this activity was an appropriate introduction.

I modeled for the students what they were to do. I placed a sheet of squared centimeter paper on a short stool in front of the class, took off my left shoe, and placed my foot on the paper. I traced around my foot, explaining as I did so that they would each do this for one of their feet.

"Then you're to figure out the area of your foot, which means finding out about how many square centimeters your foot covers," I said. "You'll notice that there are bits and pieces to think about, since your foot won't exactly cover all squares. You'll have to decide how to account for them. I know your answer won't be exact, but I'd like you to make as close an approximation as you can."

I paused for questions. Then I gave one last direction. "When you've figured the area of your foot," I said, "write an explanation to describe how you did it."

Before the students got started, I wrote the directions on the chalkboard. This not only gave me a chance to review them for the students but also gave me the chance to demonstrate how to abbreviate square centimeters. I wrote:

1. Trace around one foot (shoe off) on squared centimeter paper.
2. Figure the area of your foot and indicate sq cm or cm^2.
3. Write a description of how you did this.

When I read the students' papers that night, I found a wide variation in their written descriptions. A few were detailed and explained their thinking clearly. Nelson, for example, wrote: *I figured it out by counting the whole ones. When I was done I tried to put all the uneven squares together. I put the uneven squares together by putting a big uneven square with a small uneven square. 152 squares can fit in my foot.*

Amy's description was also clear. She wrote: *To find out the area of my foot I traced my foot on centimeter graph paper. I found out that my foot is 112 square cm.*

My method was to make a rectangle around a large group of whole centimeter squares. Then I multiplied the length times the width.

With small pieces of squares I tried to find two pieces that formed a whole. Then I put the number zero in one and the number one in the other. I would count the piece with the one in it.

In contrast, other papers were vague and unclear. Marcie, for example, wrote: *This is how I found the area in my foot. I put it in rectangles and squares and counted it that way and then added it.*

From Brian: *I counted them with meshment with a ruler.*

From Kathy: *I counted the squres that were hole then I counted the squres that were not and my foot came out to be 120½.*

I wrote comments on each paper, making suggestions for improvements. For example, on Marcie's paper, I wrote: "Why did you decide to use rectangles and squares? What did you add?" On Brian's paper, I wrote: "Please explain how you used a ruler to measure." On Kathy's, I wrote: "How did you count the squares that weren't whole? How did you keep track of what you did?"

The next day I discussed my reactions with the whole class.

"When you were figuring the areas of your feet yesterday," I said, "I noticed that you were working on solving the problem in different ways. Last night when I read all the descriptions you wrote, I found that some of you clearly reported what you did and what you were thinking. Others, however, didn't give me very much information about what you did or what you thought. If I hadn't been here with you, I wouldn't have much of an idea about the problem solving you were doing."

I explained that I had selected some of their papers to read to the class. "Without revealing your names," I said, "I'm going to read a few of your descriptions for us to discuss. I think this can help you think about improving your writing. Then I'll return your papers to you, so you can read my specific comments and suggestions and make changes."

I gave one more instruction before beginning to read. "As you listen," I said, "decide whether you get a picture of what the writer is doing. If it isn't clear, think about what might help. I'll share my ideas as well."

I began with Nelson's paper. The other students thought it gave a clear description, and I agreed. I then read Kathy's as a contrast. Her method seemed similar to Nelson's, but she didn't describe what she actually had done. "I need details in order to understand," I said.

I then read Amy's paper, which the class agreed was a clear description. I followed with Jerry's and Marcie's papers, and again we discussed what was missing.

"Remember," I told the class, "this was just your first writing assignment in math class. Writing about what you do in math will get easier with more practice."

I collected their rewrites the next day and found that most of their second attempts were indeed better. From Marcie, for example: *I first drew the biggest rectangle that would fit inside my foot. I figgered out how many squares in my rectangle by multiplying the length and the width. I combined smaller pieces together to make more wholes. The total number of whole squares were 105.*

From Brian: *I counted the full squares and then I estamated and put the halfs together and the quarters together. I got 111½.*

For an example of giving feedback in writing, see pages 71–74.

Jessica described how she marked the fractional parts of squares. (Grade 5)

First, I counted the wholes. Then, I tried to match of the thirds, fourths etc. and counted them as wholes, each time I tried to mark the wholes with crayon so I wouldn't count them again.

Total: 113

> Step 1 First, I colored all of the whole squares brown. I found the number of the brown squares and wrote it down on my paper.
>
> Step 2 Then I colored the half squares orange. I found the number of half squares and wrote it down.
>
> Step 3 After the halves I did the quarter squares. I wrote down the number and then continued. *I colored green
>
> Step 4 I then colored the three quarter squares black. I wrote down the number and I added up all of the wholes, halves, quarters, and three quarter squares. My answer was 152 ½

Jonathan gave a step-by-step description of the procedure he used to estimate the area of his foot. (Grade 5)

Feedback from Students (Grade 3)

A friend visiting my third grade class commented about how the children working on writing assignments would come to me for feedback. Often there was a line of several children waiting for me to read their work. This wasn't a system that I initiated; it just evolved as the students sought help and a response. I think that the students liked receiving immediate feedback about their papers. My friend commented that the children watched me carefully while I read what they had written and listened intently to my comments. She wondered how the children felt about my feedback.

I didn't know, so I told her I'd try to find out. I told the class about our visitor's interest and asked them to do some writing on the issue. I structured the assignment by writing four sentences on the chalkboard for them to complete:

1. Ms. Burns asks us to write because _____.
2. She accepts my paper when _____.
3. When Ms. Burns accepts my paper, I feel _____.
4. When Ms. Burns doesn't accept my paper, I feel _____.

Their responses to the first sentence revealed their perceptions of the value of writing in math class. Tanya wrote: *Ms Burns asks us to write because she wants to know what we think without us shouting out what we want to say. It helps me out because I can just jot it down, and I can read it over and change it.*

Sam wrote: *Ms. Burns asks us to write because she wants to know how we think and do things.*

Angie wrote: *Ms. Burns asks us to write because she wants to know what we think and how we think about math. Ms. Burns also wants us to write because it helps us put more thought into math.*

From Lisa: *Ms. Burns asks us to write because she wants us to know how we feel about the problems and the answers. And she wants the answer to stick in our head.*

Jenna wrote: *Ms. Burns asks us to write because she wants to see if we understand.*

From Brandon: *Ms. Burns asks us to write because she wants to know how we solved the problem.*

From Paul: *Ms. Burns asks us to write because she wants us to lern and think.*

Maria wrote: *Ms. Burns asks us to write because she wants to know why I think what I do.*

Lindsey added her usual personal twist to the sentence: *Ms. Burns asks us to write because she wants to know what is going on in our lovely little heads.*

The following were typical of the responses to the second prompt. Tanya wrote: *Ms. Burns accepts my paper when I work hard on it and write something that is sencible and something that she can understand.*

Angie wrote: *She accepts my paper when I put detail and excamples into it.*

From Rebecca: *I think she accepts my paper when it is complete, like a finished puzzle. but it also has to make sence. After it's totally complete, she will accept it.*

From Paul: *She accepts my paper when it makes sence and I think a lot abot it.*

Maria wrote: *She accepts my paper when I really concentrate on my work and make like I was going to read it myself.*

In response to the last two prompts, Angie wrote: *When Ms. Burns accepts my paper I feel two feelings, proud and relifed* [relieved], *proud because it was worth the work and relifed because (like most) I'm not in the mood for writing more. When Ms. Burns doesn't accept my paper I don't feel as proud.*

Michael wrote: *When Ms. Burns accepts my paper I feel good because I know she likes it. When Ms. Burns doesn't accept my paper I feel I should have done a better job on telling her what I think.*

> ## Writting in Math Class
>
> 1) Ms. Burns asks us to write because she wants to know what we are learning.
>
> 2) She accepts my paper when I put a lot of work into it.
>
> 3) When Ms. Burns accepts my paper I feel good because I know she likes it.
>
> 4) When Ms. Burns doesn't accept my paper I feel I should have done a better job on telling her what I think.

Michael's paper showed that he understood the purpose of the writing assignments. (Grade 3)

Rebecca wrote: *If I've writen a lot, and my hands tired, I feel good that I dont need to write more. I also feel good, because I did it right. When she doesn't accept, I usually don't mind too much. But when I'm tired I go back to my seat, and stop and rest, then things come to my mind and I can think. Then she might accept it.*

Some children, however, expressed displeasure about my not accepting their papers. Lindsey, for example, wrote: *When Ms. Burns accepts my paper, I feel happy, glad, relived, thankful, and great! When Ms. Burns doesn't accept my paper I feel sort of angry.*

Paul wrote: *When Ms. Burns accepts my paper, I feel good. When Ms. Burns doesnt accept my paper, I feel a littel like oh no I have to write more.*

Kim wrote: *When Ms. Burns accepts my paper I feel proud and happy to get to do something else. When Ms Burns doesn't accept my paper I feel made and I don't want to write anymore and when I do write more I don't do my best because my fingers are tired.*

Tanya's paper was the strongest of these. She wrote: *When Ms. Burns accepts my paper, I feel happy and relieved because I don't have to write any more because usually my hands hurt after I write alot. When Ms. Burs doesn't accept my paper I feel like crying and screaming because I can't think of anything to write and my hands <u>ache</u>. Please accept this paper.*

Tanya was clear about the purpose of writing assignments and about her feelings when her work wasn't accepted. (Grade 3)

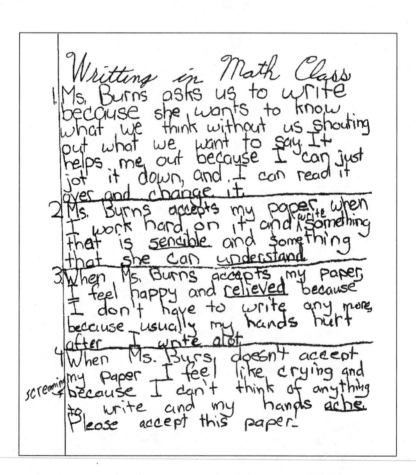

What I Know About Division (Grade 3)

At times I have children read their finished work aloud to get feedback from the rest of the class. In these instances, I let the children know in advance that they will be sharing their writing. Often I have them each prepare by first reading the paper aloud to another child for feedback before presenting it to the entire class. I encourage students to correct errors and edit their papers.

At the end of a unit on division, I asked students to write a paper about what they knew about division. I told them they'd read their papers aloud, as I wanted them to hear one another's ideas.

After each child read, I asked the class to respond to the paper. In this way, I encouraged the children to listen actively when someone read. I gave them guidelines. "Tell what you found interesting or surprising," I said, "or especially clear or confusing. I'll give my feedback as well."

Maria read from her paper: *"Division is just the opposite of Multiplacation, like 5 × 4 = 20 and 20 ÷ 5 = 4. So all you are really doing is changing it around, just like adding is the opposite of subtracting, so Multiplacation is just the opposite of Division."*

Tanya commented, "Your paper makes sense and it's a good idea." (Tanya had written that division was like subtraction, and Maria's idea intrigued her.)

Angie said, "It's very mathematical."

Josh made a suggestion. "You could include an example," he said.

Maria later added an example about sharing cookies, showing her confusion about using the notation for division.

Maria explained how she saw division as the opposite of multiplication. (Grade 3)

Michael shared the following when he read: *"I think division is life because if you were with two of your friends and you had four cookies the problem would be four divided by two and the answer would be two. Division is sharing because you can turn the problem into a sharing story so dividing is sharing."*

Brian commented, "I like that you gave an example because that helps."

Angie said, "I like that you said, 'Division is life.' That makes it seem important."

Lindsey said, "Your paper is very clear and understandable."

Brandon's paper got a laugh and most of the comments were about how he was able to deal with his brother. Brandon read: *"Division is when you have let's say five cookies and two people. They would each get two and a half cookies, and that's how you divide them fairly. And I did this with my brother before and my brother divided them by saying he gets three and I get two. But I knew we each got two and a half."*

It's important that children receive feedback on the substance of what they've written. However, just as there's no one right way to arrive at a solution in many problem situations, there's no one right way to respond to students' writing. We need to examine and assess our choices so we continue to grow in our abilities to help children learn.

Kim related division to sharing and included an example to explain her idea. (Grade 3)

What is Division?

Division is <u>sharing</u> things with people or animals so everyone will get an even amount.

If you had 17 flowers and you wanted to share the 17 flowers wit 4 people you could make four circles and pretend that the circles were the people and make little dots in the circles and pretend that they were the flowers. When everyone had the same amount of flowers and there werent enough for everyone to have another one the extra ones would be the remainder.

this is the Remainder

they each get four.

Conclusion

Although I've long believed that writing in math class gives children the opportunity to reflect on their work, think about mathematical ideas, and deepen their understanding, it wasn't until recently that I thought to find out what the children thought. I asked a class of third graders, nine of whom I had taught as second graders, to write about how writing in math class helped them. Their answers are testimony to the benefits.

Seth wrote about how writing can lead to new ideas. (Grade 3)

> ## Math-Writing
>
> When you write about your work, your ideas lead to other ideas, which lead to other ideas etc and you can use that noledge for games which lead you to new thieries about the game, which solve problems nobodys ever thought of. Plus whos going to stop you? You can write so much, you can change your prespective about probability so you can use it every day.

may

To Lee Ann, an important benefit of writing was that it helped her remember what she was thinking and learning about. (Grade 3)

Math - Writing

When I write after doing a probability game or [any math] activity. It makes me think how you can be more instrested in it. After you write the the feeling stays in you and when you do more math the writing that you did before the strategys in your writing you remember and use. When you write it makes you think harder, harder than the games itself. But when I write it helps me belive in what I think. What you write on your paper is what happens to you that day in math. What ever you write it stays in yoo. Even if you are writing a shoping list and you lose it at least you worte it down so you will remember. That is almost the same thing as writing it down in math. But this is a little bit harder.

Timmy brought his usual sense of humor to this assignment. (Grade 3)

Math - Writing

Well for one, you are not jumping on the couch. Having a ball the whole math time. because in your paper you cant say I was doing my flips on the couch the whole math time. And I also think it makes you think a whole lot more like you can tell the strategy that you figured out. And how you figured out the strategys. And I think if you think like that every day in third grade you are going to be redy for hard work and thinking. when you're older and you will get a goed job.

Math-Writing

What writing does for me is it unlocks my brain and it lets me think. But if I didn't write I would be getting nowhere. I wouldn't learn anything. I mean I wouldn't think so hard if I didn't write. I would just play the game even if I didn't know how because I wouldn't have to write. But when you write it just makes you think.

Charlie believed that writing helped him think. (Grade 3)

Math—Writing

Writing about the activetys we do in math helps me because it is easyer to explane what I think and what I did. and it is easyer for the math teacher to understand what you think and what you do. If We just went up to the math teacher and told them what we think the math teacher rite not understand unlike writing in writing I can think and make it understandable.

Molly focused on the benefit of writing to communicate with the teacher. (Grade 3)

Questions Teachers Ask

Over the past 10 years, I've presented many of the ideas in this book to teachers in workshops and at conferences. I've shared children's work and talked with teachers about their experiences having students write in math class. When I prepared to write this book, I compiled a list of questions teachers raised during my presentations and in discussions. Also, I solicited questions from 60 teachers who have had experience incorporating writing into math instruction.

Throughout this book, I respond to these questions and concerns as I look at writing in math class from a variety of approaches. In this section, I specifically address the questions asked most often by teachers. My goal is not to offer definitive answers but to provide starting points for teachers to think about and discuss how to make writing a successful and integral part of math teaching.

Q. Will time spent on having students write in math class take away time needed for learning the basics?

A. I have a two-part answer to this question. First of all, I think that the notion of "basics" needs to be thought about in its broadest sense. I do not think that the traditional notion of defining the basics as the ability to do arithmetic computations is sufficient. Children must also learn to think and reason about all topics in the mathematics curriculum. In the area of arithmetic, children should:

- know whether a problem calls for adding, subtracting, multiplying, or dividing, or some combination of these operations;

- be able to choose an appropriate method for calculating, whether it be mentally, with paper and pencil, or with a calculator;
- know how to judge the reasonableness of an answer;
- and be able to make a decision about how to use that answer.

With this expanded notion of what is basic, writing becomes a powerful tool to help children learn. Writing helps children reflect on their thinking, present what they understand, and clarify what they know and don't know. Writing is an important and valuable tool that can support students' learning in all areas of mathematics.

Q. How often do you have students write in math class?
A. It varies. Sometimes I have students keep logs and write daily about what they did in math. At other times, students write once or twice a week to solve a problem or respond to a question I raise. There's no one way that is best for all situations. My decision about how often students write depends on the math they're studying, the purpose for their writing, and their comfort with writing.

Q. Do you ever model writing for the students?
A. I model writing as often as I can. On the board, I record students' conjectures and ideas, construct prompts for writing assignments, and write directions for assignments. I frequently try to model making revisions by correcting spelling and grammatical errors or changing wording to improve what I've written.

Q. What about students who have difficulty writing? I don't want to turn them off to math.
A. Helping children learn to write is one of the basic responsibilities of school. Students need many writing experiences in order for their writing abilities to improve, and math investigations provide a ready source for writing assignments. What's important for any writing assignment is that students have something to write about and understand the purpose of communicating their thinking.

Q. I have a student who has always enjoyed math and for whom math has always his best and favorite subject. However, now that he has to write, he's turning off to math. What can I do?
A. I've also had successful math students who are quick thinkers but resist explaining their reasoning in writing. Although these students have

enjoyed success solving math problems, they often haven't been as successful in their writing pursuits. They resent being asked to do something that makes them uncomfortable and often worry that they won't be recognized for their mathematical strength.

For these students, I explain the importance of their writing to communicate with me and others about how they reason. I do my best to present their writing in a positive light, as a way to describe their thinking and extend their ideas. I want all students to understand the importance of communicating their math ideas and that math is more than getting quick, right answers. I spend a good deal of time letting students know that I value their thinking and am interested in their ideas.

Q. My students are capable of writing, but they regularly resist writing for math. What can I do?

A. I think that some students resist writing for one of two reasons. They either don't see the purpose of the writing assignment, or they're uncomfortable with what they're expected to write and don't want to be unsuccessful.

To address the first reason, I find it helpful to talk regularly with students about why I ask them to write. I talk about this a great deal at the beginning of the year, and I continue to reinforce the reasons from time to time as the year progresses.

For students who don't know what to write, the best way I know to help is to have them talk about their ideas. Verbalizing their thoughts orally is often a helpful, if not necessary, first step for children to write. If, however, a child doesn't have anything to say about a topic, that's an indication that he or she isn't ready to write and most likely needs additional experience with the mathematics we're studying.

Q. My students are writing willingly, but I'm not satisfied with the content of their papers. How can I encourage them to write deeply and clearly?

A. It takes time for students to learn what you expect from their writing. I find that it helps to use successful papers as models for students. I frequently present papers to the class—not just to praise the students who wrote them but to point out the elements of the papers that gave me insights into the students' thinking and reasoning. Typically, I talk about the specific details and explanations that helped communicate their thinking. Also, at times I've had volunteers read papers and ask other students for feedback about how they might improve their writing to present their ideas more clearly.

Q. What about very young students? How do you help them write?

A. I tell young children that what they put on their paper should help them remember what they were thinking. I tell them to use words, numbers, and pictures to explain their ideas, and I make time to have them explain to me what they've written. At times, I'll take dictation to help a child record his or her thoughts.

Q. For some of my students, English is not their primary language. I know they have ideas about the math we're studying, but they have limited ability to write in English. What can I do?

A. This problem is not specific to writing in math class, since these children need help learning to speak and write in English in all subject areas. You can have students write in their preferred language or team with other students to collaborate on explaining their ideas in English. Whatever your approach, it should be consistent with your general classroom policy and should support and encourage the learning of mathematics.

Q. Do you ever have students write in pairs or small groups?

A. I often have students work and write cooperatively, and I do this in various ways. Sometimes I ask students to talk together and then write individual papers. Sometimes I have students collaborate on one paper, and I make photocopies to file in the folders of all who contributed. At other times, I give students the choice of working alone, with a partner, or with a small group.

Q. How do you decide when to make writing assignments individual and when to have students work cooperatively?

A. I've found that individual assignments and those done cooperatively are both valuable. Individual assignments differ from group assignments in several ways. Rather than encouraging the bustle of idea exchanges that cooperative work supports, individual assignments call for more personal reflection and expression about a subject and reveal more about individual students' perspectives.

In general, when I'm specifically interested in learning what individual students think, how they might approach a problem, or what they understand about a topic, I insist that they work on their own. In contrast, when I want students to engage in a more interactive learning situation, I have them work in groups to encourage more active participation. In all situations, I communicate to students the reasons for my decisions.

Q. What sort of feedback do you write on students' papers? Do you give grades?

A. It's important to remember that student writing serves two major purposes—as a learning tool for students as they reflect on mathematics and as an assessment tool to help me learn about what students understand and how they reason. I use students' papers to help me reflect on my lessons and think of ways to support and further their learning.

That said, I think it's important that students get feedback on what they've written and, whenever possible, I prefer to do this by talking with them. Talking with students helps me better understand their thinking. I do not grade the writing that children do in math class. Their errors and misunderstandings often provide the best opportunities to spark new learning, and I do not want grades to overshadow their writing spontaneity and become a focus of their writing.

There are times, of course, when I give students assignments that I will judge. In these instances, I'm clear about the criteria for the assignment and how I will judge it. I give students ample time to do the paper, and I provide an opportunity for them to revise their work if they wish.

Q. Do you correct grammar and spelling errors on students' math writing?

A. As often as possible and in all subject areas, I point out to students how they can improve their writing. However, I do not consider their writing in math class as first drafts for eventual publication but, more typically, as windows into their thinking and understanding. My focus is more on the content of their papers than on the grammatical construction.

However, I do address their writing skills. I ask students to underline words they're not sure they've spelled correctly, and I let them know whether the words are correct. I sometimes ask students to reread their papers to insert periods and capital letters or make other grammatical corrections so that their papers communicate more effectively. And I often ask students to add additional information or details to their papers to strengthen their explanations.

Q. How do you have students organize and keep track of their writing? Do you give them notebooks, or do they write on loose sheets of paper?

A. I've tried all sorts of systems. At times I have students make journals by stapling sheets of paper together inside construction paper covers. At other times, students record on separate sheets of paper and, after I read a class set of work, I file their papers in individual folders. When I taught middle school, I bought spiral notebooks of graph paper for the students to use for all of their class work and writing.

The particular system isn't important, as long as it's clear to the students, manageable in the classroom, and makes students' writing easily accessible to the teacher. I've found that it's best for children to keep their writing in the classroom; I've had too many students lose their journals or papers when they carry them from place to place.

Q. What do you do with students' writing?
A. Once I read a class set of papers, I file them in students' individual folders, being careful to keep the papers in order so that when I read through a folder later, there is a chronological set of work. Reading a class set of work written on the same day gives me an overview of how the class as a whole responded to a particular lesson and helps me evaluate the effectiveness of my instructional choices. Reading individual students' writing done over time, however, gives me a sense of the development of each student's thinking and understanding.

Q. How do you share students' writing with their families?
A. I think it's extremely important to communicate with parents about their children's learning. I use students' writing in parent conferences and talk with parents about their children's accomplishments, progress, and needs. Also, I send students' work home. There are several ways to do this. You may have children review their work several times a year and select work for portfolios to share with their families. Or, you might send home all of the students' work at regular reporting times with cover notes explaining the nature of the work to help the parents interpret what their children have done. I realize that communicating with parents is time-consuming and demanding, but I think that it's critical that we take the time and make the effort to let parents know what their children are doing and learning in school.

Appendix

Abbreviated or expanded versions of some of the lessons in this book appear elsewhere. The list below provides sources for these lessons. For more information about each book, please see the Bibliography on page 193.

LESSON IN THIS BOOK	OTHER SOURCE
Chapter 2	
One Gorilla, pp. 14–17	*Math and Literature (K–3), Book One,* pp. 11–13
Counting Fish, pp. 17–20	*Math By All Means: Place Value, Grades 3–4,* pp. 56–66
Sharing Candy Bars, pp. 21–24	*Math By All Means: Division, Grades 3–4,* pp. 145–151; *About Teaching Mathematics,* p. 210
Dividing Cookies, pp. 21–22	*Math By All Means: Division, Grades 3–4,* pp. 49–59
Chapter 3	
The School Bus Problem, pp. 40–43	*A Collection of Math Lessons From Grades 6 Through 8,* pp. 150–156
What I Know About Percents (So Far), pp. 43–47	*A Collection of Math Lessons From Grades 6 Through 8,* pp. 170–173
Chapter 4	
Spinner Sums, pp. 53–59	*Math By All Means: Probability, Grades 3–4,* pp. 165–177; *A Collection of Math Lessons From Grades 1 Through 3,* pp. 149–159

Chapter 11

Sharing Marbles, pp. 153–155

*About Teaching Mathematics, pp. 204–205;
A Collection of Math Lessons From Grades 1
Through 3, pp. 52–53*

Chapter 12

High or Low, pp. 157–160

*Math By All Means: Probability, Grades 3–4,
pp. 152–161*

Objects in Brobdingnag,
pp. 164–167

My Travels with Gulliver

Chapter 13

Figuring Foot Area, pp. 170–173

*About Teaching Mathematics, pp. 53–54;
A Collection of Math Lessons From Grades 3
Through 6, pp. 113–128*

Bibliography

Burns, Marilyn. *About Teaching Mathematics: A K–8 Resource*. Math Solutions Publications, 1992.

_____. *A Collection of Math Lessons From Grades 3 Through 6*. Math Solutions Publications, 1987.

_____. *Math and Literature*. Math Solutions Publications, 1992.

_____. *Math By All Means: Multiplication, Grade 3*. Math Solutions Publications, 1991.

_____. *Math By All Means: Place Value,* Grades 1–2. Math Solutions Publications, 1994.

_____. *Math By All Means: Probability,* Grades 3–4. Math Solutions Publications, 1995.

Burns, Marilyn, and Cathy Humphreys. *A Collection of Math Lessons From Grades 6 Through 8*. Math Solutions Publications, 1990.

Burns, Marilyn, and Bonnie Tank. *A Collection of Math Lessons From Grades 1 Through 3*. Math Solutions Publications, 1988.

Educational Development Center. *My Travels with Gulliver*. Sunburst Communications, 1991.

Dossey, John A. et al. *The Mathematics Report Card: Are We Measuring Up?* Educational Testing Service, 1988.

Morozumi, Atsuko. *One Gorilla*. Farrar, Straus & Giroux, 1990.

National Council of Teachers of Mathematics. *Curriculum and Evaluation Standards for School Mathematics*. NCTM, 1989.

Ohanian, Susan, and Marilyn Burns. *Math By All Means: Division, Grades 3–4*. Math Solutions Publications, 1995.

Rectanus, Cheryl. *Math By All Means: Geometry, Grades 3–4*. Math Solutions Publications, 1994.

Tompert, Ann. *Grandfather Tang's Story*. Illustrated by Robert Andrew Parker. Crown Publishers, 1990.

Zinsser, William. *Writing to Learn*. Harper & Row, 1988.

Many of these materials are available from:
> Cuisenaire Company of America, Inc.
> P.O. Box 5026, White Plains, NY 10602-5026
> (800) 237-3142

Index